Ritualizing the Disposal
of the Deceased

Toronto Studies in Religion

Donald Wiebe
General Editor

Vol. 30

PETER LANG
New York • Washington, D.C./Baltimore • Bern
Frankfurt • Berlin • Brussels • Vienna • Oxford

William W. McCorkle, Jr.

Ritualizing the Disposal of the Deceased

From Corpse to Concept

PETER LANG
New York • Washington, D.C./Baltimore • Bern
Frankfurt • Berlin • Brussels • Vienna • Oxford

Library of Congress Cataloging-in-Publication Data

McCorkle, William W.
Ritualizing the disposal of the deceased: from corpse to concept /
William W. McCorkle, Jr.
p. cm. — (Toronto studies in religion; vol. 30.)
Includes bibliographical references and index.
1. Funeral rites and ceremonies. 2. Mourning customs. 3. Human body—
Social aspects. 4. Human body—Symbolic aspects. 5. Anthropology
of religion. 6. Religion and culture. I. Title.
GT3190.M43   393—dc22   2009048251
ISBN 978-1-4331-0792-4 (hardcover)
ISBN 978-1-4331-1010-8 (paperback)
ISSN 8756-7385

Bibliographic information published by **Die Deutsche Nationalbibliothek**.
Die Deutsche Nationalbibliothek lists this publication in the "Deutsche
Nationalbibliografie"; detailed bibliographic data is available
on the Internet at http://dnb.d-nb.de/.

The paper in this book meets the guidelines for permanence and durability
of the Committee on Production Guidelines for Book Longevity
of the Council of Library Resources.

© 2010 Peter Lang Publishing, Inc., New York
29 Broadway, 18th floor, New York, NY 10006
www.peterlang.com

Printed in the United States of America

Contents

Part Three: Mental Culture

Part Four: From Corpse to Concept

Acknowledgments

This monograph is a revised version of my Ph.D. thesis, prepared and submitted to the Queen's University, Belfast, in the summer of 2007. I have taken the liberty of removing a large portion of statistical data that was included in the original manuscript. I have significantly expanded on some of the finer points in the original to emphasize my arguments. Many of these can be found in the notes. Also, I conducted a sizeable amount of fieldwork during my tenure in Belfast, mainly in South and East Asia. Although, the majority of these field observations were removed in favor of the experimental evidence, I plan to include them in several forthcoming articles and chapters.

I would like to thank my supervisor Tom Lawson, who first and foremost believed in me and this project from the very beginning. He consistently pushed me to be creative as a scholar and researcher, and challenged me to the very limit of my ability with every conversation. His role as my mentor and friend is a constant reminder of why I chose academia as my profession and passion. I would like to thank Joel Mort who saw every bit of this project through from its genesis to conclusion, reading through my rough drafts and giving unlimited advice for revisions. Joel was able to bring the best scientist out of me during my tenure in Belfast. Pierce Howard, who worked with me on testing and measurement during this project, more so he helped me enjoy the capacity for learning. Noel Sheehy for jumping on board immediately in Belfast and offering more help than any postgraduate student could hope for.

In particular, a considerable thank you to Harvey Whitehouse, who single-handedly brought me to Queen's for the first cohort of students at the Institute of Cognition and Culture. I have learned so much from you through our discussions. I would like to thank Tom Davis who taught me that Religious Studies could be academic and for all the wonderful bike rides on the Blue Ridge Parkway (NC), and Iain McKillop for his generous help with the illustrations and comments in the development of this thesis. Without their supervision and mentorship it could have never been realized.

I would also like to say thank you to my family and my friends who supported me throughout my academic career and life. It would be impossible to forget my extended family at the Institute of Cognition and Culture in Belfast, Dimitris, Oratios, Steven, Emma, Claire, Gordon, Kaisa, Jen, Colin, Mitch, Jesse, Jesper, Natalie, Paulo, Graham, Shane, and Pierre. Thanks, in particular, to Armin Geertz and Jeppe Jensen at the University of Aarhus, and Jon Lanman at Oxford.

I would especially like to thank both Jason Slone and Luther Martin for taking considerable time to read my Ph.D. thesis and offer their extensive knowledge on making it better. Thank you to Don Wiebe who offered to bring this monograph to see the light of day and all the support he gave at conferences. I would like to express my sincere appreciation to Bob McCauley at Emory University for taking my work seriously, even when it was extremely rough around the edges. Thank you to Pascal Boyer for your limitless creative knowledge in regard to my research, especially for the analogies relating jazz to cognitive and evolutionary theories of culture. I would like to say a warm thank you to all of my Chairs over the last several years including Norris Frederick, James Tabor, Douglas Eckberg, Joe Stimpl, and of course Chris Parr for always sharing his wit and humor over a pint of Guinness and rugby.

I would like to express thanks to Bruce Lawrence, Tim Light, Panoyotis Pachis, Ruth Lawson, Kay Milton, Donald Haggis, O'Hyun Park, Steven Simon, Russell McCutcheon, Byron Earhart, James Sanford, Jim Peacock, Roger Corless, Brian Malley, Justin Barrett, Todd Tremlin, Dustin Byrd, Toby Johnson, David Mozina, Michael Houseman, Merlin Donald, Carl Ernst, Richard Talbert, Suzanne Mrozik, Nancy Falk, Rudy Siebert, Dan White, Bill Bjorling, Ilkka Pyysiäinen, Hugh Halman, Brian Ayers, Tobin McCafee, Svend Deal, Fred Monroe, Mark Woollen, Joe Wall, Don Braxton, Andreas Lieberoth, Ulrich Berner, Dirk Johannsen, Magnus Echtler, Eric Venbrux, Barbara Ambros, Donald Lopez Jr., Michael Puett, Axel Michaels and the "Ritual Dynamics" Project at the University of Heidelberg, and the School of Anthropological Studies at Queen's University, Belfast. Moreso, I would like to express my sincere appreciation to Bram Bessoff for support and illustration design.

Last and certainly not least, I would like to thank Dimitris Xygalatas, Robert McKenzie, Pierce Howard, Steven Hrotic, Bert Wray, Don Wiebe, the external reviewers for the Toronto Series in Religion series, my students (who were asked to painfully read early drafts), and Heidi and Nicole at Peter Lang for all the wonderful help, comments, and advice in the development of revising this manuscript for publication. The gentle reader will please forgive any errors in this monograph. I take full responsibility them.

Cheers,
Lee McCorkle
Charlotte, NC

Technical Notes

As with any comparative study, the difficulties are enormous in regard to technical vocabulary between disciplines (e.g., anthropology, history, linguistics, psychology etc.). In this monograph, I have attempted to bridge together scientific and humanistic research that until recently were worlds apart. Now that there is a significant community involved in the *cognitive science of culture*, scholars are now able to communicate across these disciplinary divisions and generate a novel approach to the study of human culture. Here I employ the American Psychological Association (APA) reference style to facilitate experimental and naturalistic studies into the research conducted by archaeologists, historians of religions, and anthropologists.

This comparative research has also left me with several hard choices in regard to dating, language, and translation between disciplinary models. Here I use the dating system (e.g., Common Era/CE, or Before Common Era/BCE) common to historians and scholars in Religious Studies and Anthropology, over dating used by Archaeologists (i.e., Before Present/BP). This is due to the fact that this monograph appears in a Religious Studies series and that audience will be more familiar with this dating system. Also, the majority of examples and evidence covered in this volume are from what scholars categorize as the "historical era." I am, however, currently writing another volume on the evolution of ritual behavior that will cover in detail pre-historical evidence from humans and other mammals.

Whenever possible, I have streamlined certain words or phrases to aid the reader. Much of the work in this volume involved historical and ethnographic primary and secondary sources in Buddhist Studies. Therefore, certain words and phrases change due to the source. Buddhism as a historical tradition evolved in no less than ten languages and numerous dialects; so, the term where it occurs is presented in the language of the source used. After which, I use the term with its Indic (typically Sanskrit/Skt) counterpart shortly thereafter. Also, I italicized and briefly defined any foreign words the first time they are used to aid the reader. If the word is commonly used and not a reference to a specific text, but a general idea, I have dropped the italics after the first instance.

Lastly, at the end of each section (Ch. 1-8), I provide a precise and concise summary of each chapter. I encourage the reader to examine the summary first and then the chapter. I believe this will especially assist the non-specialist, but also will clarify the main arguments in this monograph. At the end of Chapter 9, I provide a brief synopsis of each chapter and summation of the last chapter.

Illustrations

Pictures

Figures

Tables

Graphs

Part One

THE CULTURE OF DEATH

Chapter One

Hanging Out with Dead People

People all over the world burn, bury, cremate, pickle, mummify, wrap, wash, and decorate dead bodies. The regular disposal of dead bodies may go back to the time of Neanderthals some fifty thousand years ago or more (Mithen 1996, pp. 20-21, 198-99). Disposing of these bodies by means of ritualized actions may be just as old a practice. The same is true of performing these actions in a religious context. Buddhist adherents, for example, have throughout history performed elaborate rituals involving corpses and their remains, *even though many doctrinal/philosophical texts in Buddhist traditions explicitly state that the body and its relics should not receive any special treatment* (e.g., Strong 2004).[1]

Questions surrounding the fact that people across cultures and throughout human history feel compelled to dispose of dead bodies by means of ritualized actions and in religious contexts have interested scholars from many disciplines. Here, I intend to give a clear account of (1) precisely what kind of widespread behaviors humans exhibit when disposing of dead bodies, (2) what kind of past and extant explanations for this behavior have been proffered, (3) the reasons these explanations fall short, and (4) a model that may provide at least a start to a new and more viable explanation of the religious ritualized disposal of corpses.

---

[1] A good example of such doctrinal evidence can be found in the *Mahāparinibbāna-sutta* within the *Dīgha-nikāya*. There is compelling evidence that this text may have originally been a part of the Pāli *Vinaya* (Pāli; Skt: monastic code) portion of the *Tipiṭaka* (Pāli: Triple-Basket) (see Schopen 1997, p. 222, n. 2; Brekke 2002, pp. 5-20; Frauwallner 1956). This is important since there are very few references to disposal rituals in the Pāli *Vinaya* itself (see Schopen, pp. 204-237). Moreover, this is a historical and theoretical problem, since much of the earliest epigraphy and architectural evidence (e.g., **Sāñchī** and **Bhārhut**) supports relic worship and rituals surrounding dead bodies in Buddhist traditions.

So to begin, I will make a strong but relatively uncontroversial claim: Humans dispose of dead bodies and this cultural behavior appears to be widespread spanning time and space.

Disposal of Dead Bodies: A Cultural Phenomenon

Examples and evidence

Fifty to sixty thousand years ago, Neanderthals (*Homo sapiens neanderthalensis*) living in Europe (modern day France and Belgium) buried their dead in distinctive graves, in certain special positions with non-utilitarian grave goods (e.g., artifacts, animal parts) and with flora/fauna near or on the bodies. Some experts have questioned the validity of these finds as "burials"; however, the material evidence, debated by archaeologists and anthropologists supports the *special* disposal of corpses by Neanderthals (Parker Pearson 1999, pp. 148-49).

Five thousand years ago in ancient Egypt, kings, called *Pharaohs*, were embalmed and mummified after their death. Many of their family, slaves, and pets were buried with them to serve them in the afterlife. Today, the monuments of their disposal (pyramids) are a witness to the extreme time and resource that the culture of ancient Egypt employed.

In ancient Japan after plagues ravished the capital city of Kyoto (circa 14th century), large numbers of corpses were apparently taken to the outskirts of the city in the overlaying mountains and burnt in large groups. These mass disposals included orienting and cremating them in ways that appeared like Chinese characters (Jap: *kanji*) to observers back in the town. These burnings (sans the corpses) are re-created in the month of August every year around the city.

Around seven hundred years ago in the British Isles, a Scottish revolutionary named William Wallace (1270-1305 CE) was publicly executed in a broad display of sadism (e.g., drawn and quartered, disemboweled) by the associates of the King of England (Edward I). His limbs were sent to the four corners of the isle where they were disposed, while his head was preserved and displayed on a pike at London Tower.

In the first years of the Common Era, dead bodies were disposed of in the bogs of northwestern Europe. These corpses did not drown in the bogs; they were executed (for criminal offenses), sacrificed, or simply killed for physical and mental dysfunctions (Parker Pearson 1999, pp. 67–71). These same bodies were not thrown just anywhere; they were then disposed of by putting them in peat bogs, preserving their bodies (accidentally) for modern archaeologists.

In North America after the death of an individual, the person is typically disposed of in one of two ways (though there are many variations). First, they might be cosmetically enhanced (with makeup and surgery) and made to look like they did when they were alive. Then they are displayed in an open casket in a professional mortuary home, where their friends and family visit them. The next day they are taken to a graveyard, their casket (many times very expensive), is lowered into a grave which is enclosed by a steel vault, and then they are buried under six feet (or more) of earth.

The second way a person might be disposed of in North America is when the new corpse is burnt in a special oven (at several thousand degrees Fahrenheit), which almost completely reduces the body to chalk like dust, with a few larger bones that remain. These "cremains" are then placed in a small urn, where they may reside at a family member's home, or the dead person's cremains may be spread on the ground somewhere other than where the body was cremated.

In a large cemetery in Manila (Philippines), the amount of people that are buried there exceeds the amount of space in the cemetery. So, some humans live in this place, where they are allowed to live for free as long as they clean out the older burial spaces and place fresh corpses into them. These people live day to day next to these remains, where they leave their mortuary homes when the families of the dead visit their deceased relatives. There are other less crowded cemeteries near the city; however, the majority of people wish to have their family and friends disposed of in this *specific* place.

Scholars have found evidence which dates the deliberate disposal of early human (*Homo sapiens*) remains to more than one hundred to one hundred fifty thousand years ago at sites such as Middle Awash in Ethiopia (Clark et al. 2003). Dating back to one hundred thousand years ago at archaeological sites like Qafzeh (Israel), humans were buried with animal bones and children were placed in unique ways and (at both sites) these remains were found with certain anatomical parts (e.g., appendages, bones, crania) manipulated or missing (see Parker Pearson 1999, p. 149).[2]

When examining the evidence for the widespread disposal behavior of dead bodies by humans, it becomes clear that this disposal is not done in the most efficient manner. Rather it is done by means of stereotyped, rigid, repetitive, and goal-demoted actions that are often time consuming and costly.

Ritualized Disposal of Corpses

Widespread cultural behaviors

Not only have humans persistently throughout history and across cultures disposed of dead bodies in a deliberate manner, they have also done so in a ritualized way. The actions surrounding disposal are typically (1) rigid, (2) stereotyped, (3) repetitive, and (4) goal-demoted behaviors (see Boyer & Liénard 2006a; see Boyer & Liénard 2006b) not just random actions of disposal. The archaeological, historical, and ethnographic records clearly illustrate that humans and Neanderthals disposed of dead bodies in such ritualized customs.

In addition, bodies in Ireland where criminals were killed in grotesque ways and then thrown into bogs where they were preserved, Buddhist relics in Sri Lanka that were created out of the disposal of dead Buddhists by cremation, ancient ossuary sites in Israel where dead bodies of ancient Jews laid their dead on slabs in burial tombs, where their bones (once decomposed) were placed into "Bone Boxes," and monuments (e.g., graveyards, mausoleums, and temples) glorifying corpse remains in different parts of the world indicate that corpses were disposed of with careful intent via ritualized actions.

---

[2] Although archaeologists proffer theories on the reasons early humans were engaging in these peculiar behaviors, the material record doesn't lend itself to certainty on the issue. Nevertheless, recent advances in experimental psychology, cognitive science, and cultural anthropology (especially ethnography) may present scientists with testable, comparative hypotheses on explaining early human disposal behavior (see Whitehouse & Martin 2004; Whitehouse & McCauley 2005; and Whitehouse & Laidlaw 2007).

Ritualized behavior

In most (if not all) cultures, humans don't just discard dead bodies as they do the trash or garbage—merely a practical and simple removal to get the job done. Instead they do so by means of special kinds of measures. These procedures include disposals where individuals engage in what we might call ritualized actions or compulsions. By ritualized compulsions, I refer to those actions Boyer and Liénard (2006b) describe as having (a) specific procedures; (b) that appear to have rules; (c) are rigid; (d) are repetitive; (e) are not haphazard; and (f) are goal-demoted, meaning the actions taken do not have a functional connection to the purported goal.

Similar to Walter Burkert's "biological definition" of ritual behavior (1983, p. 23)—sans a ritual script built by religious specialists—Boyer and Liénard proffer compulsive behavior that is non-utilitarian in these types of specialized actions. In other words, prior to "full blown" ritual behavior by religious guilds and participants, individuals and groups were engaging in ritualized compulsive behavior in the material record prior to literacy and writing.

These unconnected compulsions may have perfectly suited the new literate and religious guilds in the historical era to kick-start organized doctrinal religions (see Whitehouse & Martin 2004, p. 228), by using oral, written, and performative ritual scripts in various forms to generate meaning (and thus ideological power) over individuals and groups and their naturally occurring ritualized behavior.

People all over the world engage in such a manner. Individuals and groups throughout space and time carry out a wide variety of ritualized actions that do not appear to be universal (see Metcalf & Huntington 1991). In fact, the ethnographic record supports more diversity, rather than uniformity, in disposal behavior cross-culturally (pp. 74-75). Not all of these behaviors are equal in their accompanying sensory pageantry. For example, in some groups corpses are simply placed somewhere (though still not leaving the body where it fell) without many apparent "bells and whistles;" while other groups devote enormous amounts of time and resources toward the performance of such ritualized disposal actions. All of these behaviors are interesting because, though the tokens of ritualized actions are often culturally distinct, the ritualized disposal of dead bodies appears to be a pan-human type of activity.

Archaeological evidence

The physical evidence for the disposal of corpses is abundant largely due to the enduring nature of human remains. Even modern cremation by professional experts cannot easily break down certain bones and other human remains (e.g., femur, teeth, skull, jaw, and pelvis). It is no wonder that if a body was buried, entombed, or preserved where scavengers had little if any access and where other destructive elements (i.e., water, air) were impeded from extensive decay of the remains, the material by-product of human life might be preserved rather well. In other words, the remains of cadavers don't disappear very easily—and these remnants are sufficiently abundant in culture.

What we know about ancient disposal behavior and the culture surrounding it is rather more limited. Scientists are only able to reconstruct certain types of information from the material evidence. The data seems to indicate that between fifty thousand and one hundred and fifty thousand years ago, humans and later Neanderthals began disposing of their dead by means of ritualized actions that consumed considerable time and resources.

Some scholars have theorized that small hunter-gatherers may have buried their dead to avoid potential predators in the vicinity of the group (Mithen 1996, p. 154). This, however, doesn't seem likely as a primary reason. The groups in question moved from location to location, which removed much of this type of predator threat. This in addition to the fact that disposal—ritualized disposal in particular—would cut into time for foraging and other essential necessities. This indicates that disposal would not have been helpful to these groups. It seems more prudent to conclude, considering the Neanderthal and human archaeological evidence that ritualized disposal cannot be adequately explained merely by appealing to predator avoidance.

The death of even a single member of a small band of hunters and gatherers represented a significant loss for the group possibly jeopardizing the social unit's survival. This is especially true if the dead member was an integral member of resource gathering (e.g., food, water, and shelter) or an expert who taught others in the group how to collect important resources. Neanderthals appear to have taken care of their old and sick members (p. 151), possibly showing that information retention and social bonds were important to these groups, so much so that the death of an older member of the group might have been cause for a great celebration or mourning ceremony.

Ethnographic evidence

Every year in several Asian countries, tens of thousands of individuals attend a multi-day festival that celebrates the dead in various forms (e.g., ghosts, ancestors, *buddhas*, spirits, and aborted fetuses). *The Japanese Times* has reported what can only be described as "hauntings" (by the deceased) that were documented by media/police reports as the "Festival of the Dead" (Jap: *O–bon*) grew closer. Families return home to honor their departed ancestors with living relatives. This behavior involves eating, drinking, praying, and mourning. All of these events are meant to memorialize and celebrate the dead, both past and present (see *Picture* 1.1).

Picture 1.1 Japanese Memorial Shrine during O-bon Festival

Disposal of a corpse in Japan can be a significant drain on time and resources. In some communities extensive touching of the dead body by family members, as well as many surrounding ritualized actions, are socially and culturally required. One of the more salient activities occurs after the body is cremated. Family members use special eating utensils called *hashi* (Jap: chopsticks) to pick up bone fragments left over and then they place them into a vessel/urn where the cremains are stored for future performances. The performances involved in the disposal of dead bodies in Japan may take years before these activities can be considered successful and finished, though many times ritualized actions are performed again and again *ad infinitum*.

Anthropologists have done extensive ethnographies of pre-literate and literate cultures documenting disposal behavior in each specific cultural milieu. Though some scholars have claimed various social/symbolic theories might explain ritual behavior toward dead bodies (e.g., Bloch & Parry 1982; Durkheim 1976; Goody 1962; Hertz 1960; Van Gennep 1960), none of these theories appears to *explain* mortuary behavior cross-culturally. Here Metcalf and Hunting say:

> Anthropologists have, of course, *no special understanding* of the mystery of death. *We can at best only recount the wisdoms* of other cultures, wisdoms that have found expressions in song and dance, as well as solemn rites. (Metcalf & Huntington 1991, p. 24) (my italics)

In Frazerian fashion, Metcalf and Huntington argue that current universal theories of ritualized disposal behavior fail because they are unable to circumvent and measure the diverse cultural responses to dead bodies ethnographers have presented.[3] In other words, for every similarity that might be found in the mortuary data, there appears to be just as many differences in the ethnographic record to dispute such theories. Such issues are rooted in some anthropological theorizing, since culture is typically seen as an independent agent acting upon humans as *blank slates*; therefore, producing a varied output of behavior.

---

[3] Frazierian refers to the collected work of Sir James Frazier, who compiled myth and folklore from around the world into the multi-volume work *The Golden Bough* (1911). Frazier argued that by looking at the cumulative data from around the world universal features of human culture would be revealed. Nevertheless, Frazier's volume grew to an enormous size, and later many in social and cultural anthropology used *The Golden Bough* as an argument against universals in human culture. Currently, Frazier's legacy in the field of anthropological studies is found in the Human Relations Area Files. The HRAF is a digital project designed to collect ethnographic fieldwork for local and comparative analysis of culture.

The Religious Context

General evidence

What seems plausible from the abundant archaeological evidence available is that ritualized disposal behavior was also *religious* ritualized behavior, in other words, these actions involved notions of counterintuitive agency in regard to the corpse.[4] Between two thousand and three thousand years ago, coinciding with the introduction of writing and literacy, *religious* ritualized behaviors toward the dead appear habitually in the material/historical evidence. For instance, in a two-thousand year old ancient Buddhist discovery from Gandhāra, monastic Buddhists buried special texts that had been damaged next to relics (i.e., human remains) and corpses inside burial mounds called *stūpas* (see Salomon et al. 1999).

It is peculiar that Buddhists, in particular monastic Buddhists, performed elaborate rituals toward corpses. As Gregory Schopen has noted, monastic Buddhists in the *Mūlasarvāstivāda-vinaya* did not leave dead monks where they died "unceremoniously," or simply throw them on the funeral pyre; they, in fact, performed special actions (Skt: *śarīra-pūjā*) in order to dispose of the cadavers of other members of the monastic community (Schopen 1997, p. 212).

---

[4] Throughout this monograph I employ religion (or religious) as cultural belief and behavior that appeals to what Justin Barrett (2000) and Pascal Boyer (2001) identify (and define) as minimally counterintuitive (MCI) representations. Barrett (2004) further argues that MCI concepts are predominately skewed toward agents, since concern for agency is extremely important for human survival, both in respect to predation and social relationships (pp. 22-44). As J.Z. Smith notes, anthropologists have used a similar sense of concepts concerning agents (i.e. culturally postulated superhuman beings/agents) for quite some time (see especially Tylor 1871; Spiro 1966; Lawson & McCauley 1990), reducing religion to a "subordinate taxon" of the overarching category—culture—especially in regard to institutions (2004, p. 193). I am completely in agreement with Smith that *religion* is a "second-order" concept, mainly constructed by academics (p. 194; see also McCorkle 2008b); however, I disagree with Smith's implicit (if not explicit) Durkheimian stance that culture and cultural institutions are the agents acting upon humans (see Smith 2004, pp. 193-94, 196, n. 29 & 30; see also McCorkle *forthcoming* –c). Throughout this work, I use the terms religiosity and ritualized to identify counterintuitive cultural behavior by humans. In addition, I also employ terms such as ritual to refer to scripts built by professional religious individuals and guilds and religion as a concept used by professional scholars in the academic study of religion.

According to Jared Diamond (1995), humans domesticated plants and animals around thirteen thousand years ago. When successful, this led them to eventually form large city/states that tended to be stratified politically and economically. Moreover, successful civilizations were able to pay and feed a professional military and sustain professional guilds, resulting in the rise of religious experts including experts in the religious ritualized disposal of dead bodies.

What was not entirely clear in the early human archaeological record concerning religious ritualized behavior became more so in the cultural period of the "Axial Age," when India, China, and Greco-Rome went from hunter-gatherer to agrarian and from oral culture to written culture, all between two thousand and three thousand years ago (see Jaspers 1953). Again, the cumulative evidence from artifacts and texts from this period seems to indicate that disposal of dead bodies was not only ritualized, but performed in a *religious* context as well.

For example, in the case of the Confucian *Analects*, proper etiquette toward mourning was a noted feature of the ritualized removal of dead bodies in ancient China. Extensive rules (Chin: *li*) for the performance of the disposal in regard to filial piety toward the deceased were explicitly re-enforced in texts throughout Chinese history (see Fingarette 1998; Rawski 1988, pp. 26–29).

In ancient Greek mythology, great epics (e.g., the *Odyssey* and *Iliad*), attributed to the bard Homer, provided extensive details on the nature of the gods (counterintuitive agents) and Greco beliefs concerning the afterlife. These ideals about proper disposal of corpses and the relation between the dead, the living, and the gods are explicitly religious (see especially, Goody 1962, p. 13). This is affirmed through displays of the special places (e.g., the Parthenon) and other architectural marvels in Greece including ancient burial mounds (e.g., Phillip of Macedonia's tomb) (see *Picture* 1.2). Roman ideals, beliefs, and practices can even be found in texts such as Virgil's *Aeneid* and in later writings by Roman historians (e.g., Suetonius, Tacitus, and Pliny).

In central Asia, Buddhists in the aforementioned Gandhāra example (dated to the first–second century CE) were engaged in ritualized disposal of sacred texts that embodied special agency. When the books became damaged they appeared to require burial like humans (see Salomon et al. 1999;

Schopen 1997, 2004).[5] This Buddhist behavior is an explicit example of ritualized performance in a religious context resulting in the accumulation of artifacts (e.g., relics, burial complexes, and ritual manuals) that document disposal of bodies in the ancient world.

Picture 1.2 Phillip of Macedonia's Tomb, Greece

This *religious* ritualized disposal of corpses remains widespread and persistent throughout the comparative historical record. Most Christians believe that a man named Jesus was crucified two thousand years ago in a small province of the Roman Empire and was taken by his associates to a burial tomb. This man was executed as a criminal by the state. Most people at the time were left hanging on the crucifix, left for the dogs and scavengers as a public display of the penalty for treason against Rome (Crossan 1995, pp. 123-26). Nevertheless, according to some traditions, this *special* man was taken off the cross

---

[5] It is of special note that, in the region where the **Gandhāran** example flourished (modern day Afghanistan/Pakistan), damaged or old Qur'ans are ritually buried in special graveyards in modern times (see Pennington 2006).

by his followers and laid in a tomb (as cultural custom demanded) only to counterintuitively rise from the dead three days later.

According to widespread Christian beliefs, the man (described earlier) died for their transgressions (sins) and the only way to a special place where believers go when they die (heaven) is through the belief in the dead man, now alive eternally. Many of the man's followers are asked by special experts in this tradition to perform special actions that involve the eating of a wafer and the drinking of wine from a special cup, which symbolizes the eating of the dead man's flesh and the drinking of his blood. By doing so, many of these people are members/followers of an ongoing tradition to the dead man. In performing these special actions, followers do not consider themselves participants in cannibalistic behavior. Instead, they have earned the right to be with the departed man when the members die themselves and live forever in a place called heaven.

In parts of the Middle East, individuals have performed special actions for centuries celebrating the death of a special man (saint) named Imam Hussain. The practices by these individuals include the violent act of self-flagellation by chains, cutting their foreheads with blades, and speaking out loud their allegiance and devotion to a monotheistic God named Allah as they walk in the steps of the murdered Imam.

On the world's rooftop of the Himalayas, ritual experts hack corpses into pieces while the family of the deceased stand by (near birds of prey that will eat the remains), in another violent ritualized display of disposal known as a "Tibetan Sky Burial." Tradition holds that the body is nothing more than a container for the soul, which will be reborn into another container shortly (reincarnation) based upon the cumulative actions (Skt: *karma*) of the many lives the soul has embodied (transmigration). The body is fed to the birds of prey as a sign of good merit for other living things. The body is not, however, randomly disposed of to feed the predators, even though it is considered to be nothing more than a vessel and of no real further concern.

In several Asian countries today the disposal of some corpses is marked by a set of actions that end in the cremation of the body by fire. The cremains are then used in another set of proceedings, different from the first, whereby the remnants are entombed in a burial place. These cremains are sometimes used to perform future ritualized actions in funerals as well as rituals involving living participants. The remains might, for example, be laid upon an individual's body relieving them of their transgressions in the world. During these ritual performances the cremains are considered neither dangerous nor toxic to the participants (although they are considered supernaturally powerful). Participants offer prayers to the relics for themselves and their family members. Here is a version of such a ritual I observed recently in North America.

What Buddhists say, is not what Buddhists do

I was invited to attend a relic ceremony in North America at a Vietnamese Buddhist temple. The relics were advertised as the remains of the historical Buddha, several of his favorite disciples (including Śāriputra), and other important Buddhist saints. At the entrance I was greeted by an American in his late forties to early fifties with jeans and a button down and a long walking stick in his hand. He looked like a bohemian; someone who might have been a hippie in college back in the sixties. He invited the group I was in (which included many of my former students) to join a Buddhist community and in a very explicit but subtle way stated that, "Buddhism is a philosophy, you know, not a religion." We then entered the temple complex.

The complex itself was comprised of a courtyard with several buildings on the away side. A concrete sidewalk led to the front of one small building, where I could smell the savories of curry and other Vietnamese culinary delights. At this same spot, sat a long table where various pamphlets with reference to the relics and the mission to eventually install them in a great, golden *stūpa* in India. There was a small cigar box where donations were accepted. I placed a twenty dollar note inside the box. Many of my students placed various notes and change inside the box. This in itself was interesting, since the location of the box required a little more effort by the donor to give money. The box itself was nothing more than an old cigar box filled with different denominations of money. I remember thinking to myself that I abhor giving money to religious and political groups; yet, I and many of my students had no problem giving it to this specific group on this *special* day.

After I picked up a brochure, immediately in front of us were a collection of hundreds of shoes. I thought to myself, "Oh! We must be on sacred ground." We all removed our shoes, which were right at the stairs of two buildings. The one directly in front of us (according to my nose) was most likely the kitchen. The building slightly to the left, where the majority of the people were congregated, was the main temple, the principal space of the complex. Before we entered the temple, to the left facing the temple, was a statue (approximately 10 feet tall and made of marble) of the *bodhisattva* Avolokitś-vara. In front of this statue was a collection of flowers, small pictures, and small rolled pieces of paper, which I was told contained prayers for individuals who were ill. I viewed the statue for several minutes, marveling at the artist's craft and design. Similar to *hermes* in Greece and the *lingams* in India that I have seen, this representation of Avolokitśvara appeared absolutely sublime in its artistic form. I am sure the Buddhist community was very proud of it; since, it rivaled anything I have seen in numerous Asian countries.

Upon entering the temple (which was packed), I noticed a great deal of diversity in the people who had come to see the relics. The place was full of Vietnamese and other people of Asian descent; however, it was also full of Caucasians and Afro-centric North Americans. I recognized a great deal of people from various universities around town. I wasn't exactly sure how this relic ritual would proceed. However, after a few minutes of orientation, it flowed along pretty much like other relic rituals I had seen, and for that matter weddings and funerals.

From the inside of the temple, standing in a crowd at least ten deep, we faced several monks on our left, the relics on a table encased within glass cases in the center (slightly right), and seated were a group of what I considered to be important guests on the far right. On the back wall, which was pretty minimum in decoration, were two electric portraits of *bodhisattvas*. I was struck by the electric portraits, because they were similar to electric "beer signs" in many of the local bars and restaurants touting various beer products such as Budweiser. I joked to myself that Budweiser must have really come from "Budda-weiser, the enlightened one of all beers." All jokes aside, I found it interesting that here we were in the presence of ancient remains that were hundreds if not thousands of years old and yet, the religion had embraced novel approaches to conduct religiosity in the modern world. The inclusiveness of such an approach did not go unnoticed by the rest of the group as well.

The ceremony surrounding the relics began with a few prayers that were conducted in Vietnamese. The local monks handed out pieces of paper with the words in transliterated Vietnamese. Many of the songs repeated parts over and over (a chorus); so, it was easy to sing along regardless of whether you spoke Vietnamese or not. In between several of these Vietnamese prayer songs, the Tibetan monks chanted prayers in Tibetan and Sanskrit. In fact, it was notable because the crowd stopped at certain times, regardless of language background, and then the Tibetan monks began their chanting without missing a beat. The crowd all bent their heads in prayer. How the crowd knew to do this all at the same time was puzzling. Later, I figured that people are so psychologically tuned into *special* ceremonies like this, that they were able to connect bits and pieces of information together in a somewhat coherent thread.

After the Tibetan monks had chanted, we were told (in English) that the two nuns (Tib: *a ni*) in charge of the relics (Tib: *rjes shul*; Skt: *śarīra*) (their handling and transportation) were going to tell us the history of the relics. We were informed that these were in fact relics of the historical Buddha, Śāriputra, and other very important Buddhist saints (many of them Tibetan). Several of the more auspicious characteristics of the relics were that they appeared in various colors and that some of them were "apparently" growing. We were told that they held all kinds of powers and that after their tour around the world they would in fact be laid into a golden *stūpa* in India. The nuns, themselves, were very educated in the history of these relics. I did find it amusing that they were in fact traveling around America in that old conversion van outside the entrance. I had a hard time convincing myself that if Jesus, St. Peter, or St. Paul's remains were ever found, Christians in America would allow the remains to travel in a beat up conversion van. In fact a bit later I learned the extent of extreme care the "Dead Sea Scrolls" traveled to America. Of course, there was a significant amount of money involved in their travels as well.

After the nuns finished with their historical introduction we were then offered a *Dharma* (Tib: *chos*; Buddha's teaching) reading by a young monk (Tib: *grwa pa*). The monk's reading was what can only be described as a grade school lesson on the Buddha's teaching. "The Buddha (Tib: *sangs rgyas*) is the doctor, the Dharma is the medicine, and the *Saṃgha* (Tib: *dgon sde*; community of believers) are the nurses." I had seen this technique before in Buddhist texts; however, what most interested me was that it appeared that only a monk (male) was able to give it, though the content was elementary by any normal sense. The transition between the nuns and the monk was clearly demarcated. In addition, it was implicitly obvious that there was a tension between the nuns, who were in charge of such delicate and important objects, yet they were not allowed to give an elementary teaching of the Buddha, suggesting that there were caste (Tib: *rigs*) restrictions in place—a teaching that any child familiar with the *Jātaka Tales* (stories of the Buddha's former lives, many times as an animal) could have given.

After the *Dharma* sermon (Tib: *chos bshad*), several of the invited guests (who wore the robes of Tibetan Buddhists) spoke shortly on the meaning and philosophy of the relic ceremony. The crowd was told that, "only one prayer" per person was allowed due to the number of visitors. We were told to form a line and circumambulate (clockwise) the relics on the table and then a monk would raise the relics (only one case) over the participant's head. Then the monk would gently touch the case (containing the relics) to the person's head. After the ritual performance, the participants could exit and could eat the prepared Vietnamese cuisine in the other building.

One of my informants (Hu) described this ritual as an "awakening" experience. Here Hu told me that he "circumambulated the relics and saw (pointed out by several monks) the strange colors of the relics: purples, greens, reds, and oranges." The relics did indeed appear to have grown, or melted into various "auspicious" pearl like stones. After his circumambulation, Hu knelt down and the monk laid the relic case on his forehead. Hu described this moment as "electricity flowing through my body. I felt like all of my past misdeeds had been wiped away. I felt like a new person."

I participated in the ritual myself and didn't have the same experience as Hu; however, I found it exciting that participants all around me were exhibiting similar behavior and emotions that Hu had. I remember thinking that maybe I didn't perform the ritual the correct way and therefore didn't have the same outcome. I took enjoyment in the fact that maybe I had no bad karma to wipe away; albeit, I know better than that. In addition, the people performing the relic ritual were almost contagious to each other in their emotional happiness. I saw at least five people erupt in various outbursts, only to have someone respond with an emotional answer. It almost struck me as someone who observes the transmission of a yawn in a small population. Many times, when you see someone yawn, it will go around the room as if it is an epidemic of yawns, one after another, whether consciously or unconsciously people will just yawn for no apparent reason. The emotional excitement concerning the touching of the relics appeared on the surface eerily similar to the contagiousness of yawning.

What is most interesting is that the people were not in fact touching the actual relics. Many times books in ancient Buddhism were worshipped and you can see that they were never read. This is due to the millions and millions of times they have been touched, which wear the pages down, where you can't possibly read the words contained within them. Participants, including Hu, were having an arousing experience by touching the container that holds the relics, not the relics themselves. In the participants' minds, the container assumed all the properties of the relics themselves. I asked Hu if the ritual would have been successful with just the container that held the relics. He replied, "probably so," and then later affirmed that "yes," the containers would have elicited the same basic end result." Though he also added "it might not of (sic) been as powerful."

I asked Hu about the act of the monk touching his forehead, when he felt the "electricity" go through his body. I asked him what (agency) provided the current that he felt. He responded that, "the relics cause the electricity." I then asked Hu what the role of the monk handling the relic case was. He responded that, "I think the monk is just a vehicle for the relic and its power." I then asked him if the monk was important to the ritual. He responded that, "the monk isn't needed," though he thought the monk probably gained "special powers" from touching the relic case. I asked Hu if he thought he had special powers now that he had touched the relic case. He said he wasn't sure. Nevertheless, he felt "spiritually cleaned" by it.

What is interesting about these particular observations is that Buddhism is a tradition consistently used in the comparative study of religion as a *straw man* to argue that it is not necessary to have a definition of religion containing the notion of supernatural counterintuitive beings/agents and ritualized behavior toward them. Moreover, "true" Buddhism (here referring to what some individuals construe as "original" or early Buddhism) is constantly held up as a religious tradition that is devoid of superstitious behaviors especially including religious ritualized actions involved in the disposal of dead bodies. Any participation of such performances is explained as *heretical, folk, later, Mahāyāna*, and *superstitious* Buddhism. All of these arguments about religious ritualized behavior (mainly about dead bodies and their remains) are explained away as something foreign to the "real" Buddhism.

Summary

In Chapter One, I argued that the ritualized compulsion to dispose of dead bodies appeared early (one hundred and fifty thousand years ago) in the human material record. It also seems that Neanderthals engaged in disposal behavior around fifty thousand years ago. These widespread special disposals were most likely not in regard to predator avoidance, as some scholars have suggested. As the material (e.g., archaeological) evidence became more abundant and large-scale societies grew more complex with the introduction of domesticated plants and animals, these disposals appeared more elaborate over time. Although there have been significant hypotheses on the reasons for such special performances, the growing body of ethnographic evidence has not supported a universal theory of disposal behavior by humans.

In this chapter, I used examples and evidence to argue that the historical rise of professional guilds of religious and ritual experts—which occurred only in the last few thousand years—led to the generation of ritual scripts used to connect counterintuitive behavior in regard to dead bodies by individuals and groups. Through oral and written texts and artifacts, these religious experts utilized such salient disposal behaviors and counterintuitive assumptions concerning corpses into coherent portraits of meaning. In doing so, religious guilds became very powerful custodians of a "religious disposal repertoire" that allowed them ideological power over political and social authority, which increased over historical time. Moreover, many of the large religions of the world gained their appeal by opportunity through trade and especially ideological control over disposal behavior.

In particular, the religious tradition(s) of Buddhism spread as a small Indian sect in the Gangetic Plain throughout greater Asia precisely because of the specific attention that was paid to ritualized disposal behavior by individuals and groups. Although Buddhism is often used as the example *par excellence* against an *intellectualist* argument for a definition of a religion (i.e., supernatural agents), the role of dead bodies and their remains as supernatural (counterintuitive) agents has long been and remains a salient ritual tool in Buddhist practice throughout the world.

Chapter Two

Manufacturing Buddhism

Recently, in Charlotte, NC (US), a Buddhist monk immolated (suicide by burning to death) himself in an act of protest against Vietnamese religious persecution.[1] In an interview with a local paper, the senior monk of the temple responded that a religious expert, trained in the doctrines of Buddhism, needed to get together with the community to decide what to do with the cremated remains of the dead monk (Merrill 2003; Moore 2003).

Historically in Buddhist traditions, dead bodies have been cremated in practices dating back to the ritual disposal of corpses in ancient India, which pre-date Buddhism in South Asia. Many texts in ancient India assert that the body means rather little; it is of no consequence since it is a container for the *ātman* (Skt: kernel; soul, spirit). This can be seen explicitly, not only in the philosophical texts of ancient and classical Buddhism, but also in the beliefs of modern monastic Buddhists like the Tibetan spiritual leader, the Dalai Lama. In particular, South Asian Buddhist philosophy advances the theory that a sentient being is a cluster of forms or aggregates (Skt: *skandha*) that are an illusion. Therefore, the body (container) is an illusion as well. This philosophical approach in Indian Buddhism is known as the theory of *anātman*, or no-self.[2]

This ambiguous attitude toward dead bodies points to a contradiction in Buddhism, since, despite Buddhist doctrines stating that the body–especially a dead body–is of little consequence (Akira 1990, pp. 43-45), the cadaver is, nevertheless, treated as something quite significant in Buddhist practice both historically and in modern Buddhist communities. In other words, *Buddhists emphasize the very thing (the body/remains) that Buddhist doctrines say is of no or lit-*

---

[1] This was quite detrimental to the Vietnamese Buddhist community in Charlotte, since the monk was a very prominent member of the temple.

[2] For an extended summary of this philosophy see Rahula (1974, pp. 32-33).

tle importance (see Strong 2004; see L. Wilson 1996). The point is that the doctrine does not conform to Buddhist practice. Actually, Buddhists perform explicit special actions towards dead bodies much of the time. In fact they create monuments that glorify these remains (see *Picture* 2.1).

Picture 2.1 Monument/Burial Mound to Commemorate Ground
Zero/World War II (Hiroshima)

The Generation of a World Religion

Buddhism presents a problem for the study of comparative religion. As I have already stated, the tradition known as Buddhism was (and is) exploited by scholars of religion to debate the defining traits of religion. Namely, that to be considered a religion, a set of ideas and practices must contain the belief in gods (i.e. supernatural beings). The extant Pāli tradition holds that in "original" Buddhism (here meaning the tradition and texts preserved by followers of the Theravāda), the Buddha himself taught his community that the belief in spirits and gods was unfruitful for liberation from the "wheel of suffering"

(Skt: *saṃsāra*) and that his body was not to be adorned or worshipped after his death (Akira 1990, p. 36). Here, according to the tradition, the Buddha says:

> Do not hinder yourselves, Ananda, by honoring the remains of the Tathagata.... There are wise men, Ananda, among the nobles, among the brahmans, among the heads of houses, who are firm believers in the Tathagata; and they will do honor to the remains of the the Tathagata.

> [W]rap the body...in a new cloth. When that is done they wrap it in a carded cotton wool. When that is done they wrap it in a new cloth, and so on till they have wrapped the body in five hundred successive layers of both kinds. Then they place the body in an oil vessel of iron, and they cover that close up with another oil vessel of iron. They then build a funeral pyre of all kinds of perfume, and burn the body....And then at the four cross roads they erect a stupa. *Mahāparinibbāna-sutta* 5.11 (Ling 1981, p. 187)

The text clearly illustrates the Buddha's explicit burial instructions to his faithful disciple Ānanda; however, it is intriguing that the Buddha tells Ānanda not to perform these actions himself. Many Buddhist scholars and Buddhists themselves regard this passage as the starting point for the belief in a division between a non-theistic (and therefore non-religious), monastic Buddhism and a religious laity.

This is a peculiar notion since modern Buddhists regularly engage in ritualized behaviors that incorporate spirits, gods, ghosts, and dead Buddhist saints. In fact, in the Pāli *Vinaya* (i.e. monastic code), the historical Buddha engaged in behavior that can be regarded as superhuman or at least counterintuitive behavior not typical of humans. Here the writers of the Pāli *Vinaya* state:

> At the command of the Blessed One the five hundred pieces of fire-wood could not be split and were split, the fires could not be lit up and they were lit up, could not be extinguished and were extinguished; besides he created five hundred vessels with fire. Thus the number of these miracles amounts to three thousand five hundred. *Mahāvagga* I, 20.24 (Rhys-Davids & Oldenberg 1996, pp. 133–34)

Thus, according to the tradition taken from the extant Pāli *Vinaya*, the historical Buddha is not to be worshipped or adorned, yet he is able to instantiate superhuman behavior when pressed or angered.[3] This same type of "theo-logical incorrectness" (see Barrett 1998; see Slone 2004) to the Buddha's corpse and relics is also found within the Pāli *Vinaya*. The Buddha explicitly states in the previously mentioned *Mahāparinibbāna-sutta* (5.1) (Pāli; Skt: *Mahāparinirvāṇa-sūtra*) that his body is not to be adorned after his death; this was the job of the lay community, not the monastic community (Ling 1981, pp. 187–88). Here Akira Hirakawa says:

> [W]hen the Buddha was about to die, he told Ānanda that the monks and nuns were not to conduct a funeral service over his remains....As for his re-mains, the Buddha stated that "Brahmans with deep faith and worthy householders would pay reverence to the remains...." Thus from the very be-ginning, *stūpas* were protected and maintained by laymen, and laymen did homage at them. (Akira 1990, p. 271)

Nevertheless, there is almost no reference to the monastic rules in the Pāli monastic codes on *how* to handle a body *post mortem*. Only these two brief ref-erences on what action should be taken with the deceased possessions.[4] Here the (Pāli) *Vinaya* says:

> Now at that time two Bhikkhus were journeying along a high road in the country of Kosala. And they came to a certain residence, and there one of the two fell ill. Then the *Bhikkhus* there thought: "Waiting upon the sick has been highly spoken of by the Blessed One. Let us then, friends, now wait upon this Bhikkhu." And they waited upon him, and while he was being nursed by them he completed his time [died]. Then those Bhikkhus took the Bhikkhus bowl and his robes, and went to Sāvatthi, and told the matter to the Blessed One. On the death of a Bhikkhu, "O Bhikkhus, the Samgha be-comes the owner of his bowl and of his robes. But, now, those that wait upon the sick are of much service. I prescribe, O Bhikkhus, that the bowl and the set of robes are to be assigned by the Samgha to them who have waited upon the sick...."Now there came a time a certain Bhikkhu who was possessed of much property, and a plentiful supply of a Bhikkhu's requisites, completed his time... the set of robes and the bowl are to be assigned by the Samgha to them who have waited upon the sick. And whatever prop-

---

[3] See also Roger Corless' *The Vision of Buddhism* for further supernatural behavior attributed to the Buddha (1990, p. 190) and Brekke (2002, pp. 28–30).

[4] There is another brief reference in the regulations concerning *bhikkhunīs* (Pāli: nuns); how-ever, it follows the same pattern as the regulations concerning monks. See the *Kullavagga* 11.1 in (Rhys-Davids & Oldenberg 1998b, pp. 343–44).

erty...that is to be divided by the Samgha that are present there, but whatever large quantity of property...this is not to be given away. *Mahāvagga* VIII, 27.1-5. (Rhys-Davids & Oldenberg, 1998a: 243-45)

The second reference regarding dead bodies and their property is in response to the "mishandling" of the robes by a member of the community of believers (Skt: *Samgha*). Here the *Vinaya* says:

"Give this robe to such and such a Bhikkhu;" and he, whilst on his way, hears that the Bhikkhu who sent it is dead; then if he keeps the robe himself as a robe of a deceased Bhikkhu, it is rightly kept; if he takes it himself in trust on the one to whom it was sent, it was wrongly taken. *Mahāvagga* VIII, 31.2 (Rhys-Davids & Oldenberg, 1998a: 252-53)

Notice that the references in the *Vinaya* rules are concerned with the dead monk's (Pāli: *bhikkhu*) possessions (e.g., robes, bowls, and wealth), not the actions to be performed to the corpse. This is somewhat unusual since early material evidence circa second/third century BCE onward (e.g., Sāñchī, Bhārhut, Amarāvatī, Mathurā, and Nāgārjunakoṇḍa) supports the special handling of relics of the Buddha and Buddhist saints, and in addition, the production of monastic complexes that handle the ritual disposal of dead bodies.

It appears that the entire point of the Buddha's (and other Buddhists) instructions is to transform the living person (now dead) into a continuous and transcendental representation made present by the relic, which is subsequently incorporated into future disposal actions. To use Arnold Van Gennep's systemization of the "rites of passage," the ritual's purpose is to separate the biological corpse and then to transform its relics into a "new state" (Strong 2004, p. 3; e.g., Van Gennep 1960, p. 146; see also J. L. Watson 1988a, p. 235). The purpose of this state, according to some scholars (e.g., Durkheim, Hertz, and Bloch), is to strengthen the social organism and re-enforce these salient representations *ad infinitum*. Strong goes on to call attention to the problem of relics stating that, "In the Theravāda world, according to Buddhaghoṣa (fifth century CE), possession of a relic was one of the definitional criteria for what constituted a proper monastery..., and still today, relics of the Buddha are found in virtually every community, sometimes in very large numbers" (Strong 2004, p. xiv).

Material Culture and Mistaken Identities

At one of these monastic complexes (e.g., Sāñchī), dated to sometime in the second-third century BCE (Harle 1994, p. 32), the material evidence contains burial mounds called *stūpas* (Skt; Pāli: *thūpas*), which contain the remains of special Buddhists inside them. This is certainly not evidence to argue that Buddha himself engaged in this behavior, since it is argued by scholars that he lived from one hundred to several hundred years prior to the dating of Sāñchī and other early South Asian complexes (Brekke 2002, pp. 11-20; Frauwallner 1956: p. 54; Rhys-Davids & Oldenberg 1998a, pp. xxii-xxiii).[5] However, there would likely be rules governing such disposal, given that (according to this same tradition) several of the historical Buddha's favorite followers preceded him in death (Robinson & Johnson 1982, p. 32).[6] Nevertheless, these arguments are a red herring to the problem of ritualized behavior by participants who call themselves Buddhists. Religious systems rarely, as ethnographic observations attest and historical studies confirm, remain in an ideological vacuum of their founder's beliefs and practices as presented in texts.[7]

Many scholars of religion in the twentieth century argue that the belief in spirits, worship of *stūpas*, and other kinds of supernatural behavior(s) is in fact the problem of a "pristine" Buddhism versus the "heretical" practices of lay

---

[5] Though as Gregory Schopen (1997) has argued extensively, the Buddha, when asked (by Ānanda) about his funeral arrangements in the Pāli *Mahāparinibbāna-sutta*, "*katham mayam bhante tathāgatassa sarīre paṭipajjāmāti*," ("How are we to conduct ourselves in regard to the body of the Tathāgata?"), in the Pāli *Mahāparinibbāna-sutta* and other versions of this story he replies, a *stūpa* is to be erected at a main crossroad after the "worshiping of the body" (Pāli: *śarīra pūjam kṛtvā*) (pp. 102, 105-57 respectively). After his cremations and the worshipping of his body (*śarīra pūjā*), a *stūpa* was erected. Therefore, Schopen adds that, "[t]he construction of a *stūpa*...signaled the end of *śarīra pūjā*, not its beginnings" (p.108). Ergo, Buddhist monks were involved in what might be deemed as "religious" behaviors prior to any relic cult that might have existed, though it seems fairly reasonable to argue that Buddhists were involved in behaviors with pre-existing relic cults (Decaroli 2004, pp. 56-86).

[6] In fact Stupa II at Sāñchī is said to contain the relics of the Buddha's favorite disciples, Śāriputra and Maudgalyāyana (see Harle 1994, p. 34; see Strong 2004, p. 206), which, in theory, their funerals predate the Buddha's death (Skt: *parinirvāṇa*). This may indicate that the Buddha sanctioned ritualized disposal during his lifetime.

[7] Carol Anderson (1999) cogently argues that even "The Four Noble Truths," considered by many Buddhists and scholars as authoritative teachings of the historical Buddha, may in fact be the product of Buddhist traditions centuries later (see p. 230).

people. These lay behaviors, characterized in classical philosophical texts like "The Diamond Sutra" (Skt: *Vajracchedikā-sūtra*), refer to the lay "corruption" of an "original" Buddhism as the "foolish common people" (Skt: *pṛthagjanata*). Here the author(s) of the text say:

> "Seizing of a self," as no-seizing. Subhuti, has that been taught by the Tathagata [The Buddha]? And yet the *foolish common people have seized upon it.* "Foolish common people," Subhuti, as really no people have been taught by the Tathagata. Therefore are they called "foolish common people?" (Conze, 1958: 136) (my italics and brackets)

The writers of the passage seem to imply that there are those who follow the Buddha's teaching and others who are simply "foolish." According to this passage, the "foolish common people" (Skt: *pṛthagjanata*) must claim to have been taught the Buddha's teaching.[8] This is a direct polemic toward those "at-

---

[8] It should be noted that the term *pṛthagjanata* is used for a variety of reasons in Buddhism. Although in South Asian Buddhism it could refer to either lay person (believer or non-believer) or monastic, the influence of later Chinese Buddhism typically defines a *pṛthagjanata* as a person who has not reached a certain "level" of spiritual attainment. Nevertheless, the term predates Buddhism and may have been a common concept during the Upaniṣad period (circa 800–200 BCE) in ancient India, referring to Vedic recitation groups, who memorized oral texts but didn't understand the meaning of the texts (for modern analyses of these groups, see Staal 1989 and Parry 1994). This is significant, according to traditional history, due to members of the early Buddhist *Saṃgha* who were of the Brahmin caste. According to many traditions in early/sectarian Buddhism, recitation of oral texts (e.g., *sūtra*, *vinaya*, and *abhidharma*) was performed by professional recitation experts who formerly had expertise in Vedic and similar Indic religiosity. Staal (1979) argues that recitation of Vedic texts involved memorization techniques that required no semantic comprehension of the texts themselves; yet, they contained a precise syntax. Parry (1994), offers that *Brahmins* (Skt; Vedic ritual experts) in Banaras, offer limitless interpretations of ritual performance (pp. 1–2, 33–34); however, no such universal, intrinsic meaning is apparent in his ethnography. This suggests that semantic comprehension is not a pre-requisite for *proper* and *successful* recitation of the oral texts and the performance of the rituals associated with them (see also Goody 1987).

It is difficult to discern whether the *Vajracchedikā-sūtra* was originally an Indic text or whether it was created in China and made to appear as if it was an Indic (and thereby a possibly older) creation (see Nattier 1992, pp. 153–223 for a powerful argument on the Chinese origins of the *Prajñapāramitā* Hṛdaya, commonly known in English as "The Heart **Sūtra**"). It would seem that sections of the text are likely Indic and from earlier oral traditions. During the rise of the groups that preceded **Mahāyāna** (e.g., "the cult of the book"), many comparable texts to the *Vajracchedikā-sūtra* were written down and copied but not read. They were used as texts that carried special (supernatural) agency. It is, however, probable that these groups used the texts

tached" to the literal teachings or sayings of the Buddha.[9] Nevertheless, some of these early texts are deceiving because they contain polemics that appear in one instance to be pro-monastic (against the laity) and in the other instance appear to be anti-monastic (against a certain faction of the monastic community). As in another passage from the *Vajracchedikā-sūtra*:

> Moreover, Subhuti, the *spot of earth where this sutra will be revealed, that spot of earth will be worthy of worship* by the whole world with its gods, men, and Asuras, worthy of being saluted respectfully, worthy of being honored by *circumambulation*, like a shrine will be that spot of earth. (Conze 1958, p. 131) (my italics)

The text here is misleading. On one hand it appears to use a polemical genre to criticize one group of people who are "common," meaning not of the monastic community. Nevertheless, a closer look reveals that these are monastic writers criticizing others (probably elders) in the monastic community. Moreover, this group advocates the worship of a text at a certain location, which is to be circumambulated, such as *stūpas* at ancient complexes in India (e.g., Sāñchī and Bhārhut in the north, Amarāvatī, and Nāgārjunadakoṇḍa in the south). This presents a conundrum since the actions of this monastic example seem to mimic perceived notions of "superstitious" lay behavior (i.e., worshiping texts and *stūpas*).

But is there a real distinction between the behavior of the writers of this text and superstitious behavior via a lay environment? Why would the monastic community have different ideals and behaviors from the lay community? The answer might be surprising. I will argue that both monastic and lay communities employ similar, if not identical, mental systems concerning religious behavior. I will also argue that this behavior is (1) natural to the majority of human beings (including Buddhists), (2) involves many kinds of references to

---

and terms like *pṛthagjanata* as a polemic to promote their differing views on the nature of the Buddha and *buddhavacana* (Skt; literally, what the Buddha said or, traditionally, what the Buddha taught).

[9] This would seem a direct reference to monastic Buddhists who were fixated on the Buddha's teaching through the application of mnemonic guided oral texts. This was common practice for the remembrance of large oral texts in ancient India. See (H. Falk 1990; Lopez Jr. 1995; Staal 1989). See also McCorkle, (*forthcoming–b*) for a discussion in regard to the vertical and horizontal transmission of oral texts in early Indian religions and Indic ritual behavior.

superhuman agents, (3) involves the activation of certain psychological systems that inform human behavior regardless of religious training, and (4) that these systems are successfully triggered by and inform human behavior, especially as it pertains to perceptions and material representations concerning death, dead bodies, and the remains of corpses.

Are Religious Experts Really That Different from the Laity?

Historians of religions theorize that the problem of a monastic/lay difference is due to the fact that doctrines are primarily written by a small number of elites, and the vast majority of participants of any particular religion simply don't know the doctrines of their respective traditions. Because of this view, more recent research in the *history of religions* discipline has focused on the actual views and practices of religious participants and have favored anthropological "thick descriptions" (e.g., Geertz 1973) of ritual acts to understand specific features of religious traditions, rather than a purely textual analysis of religious ideas and behaviors influenced by Protestant Christianity (Gombrich 1988, pp. 172-97; Silk 1994, pp. 171-96).

Gregory Schopen has persuasively argued that analysis of both textual materials *and* other material evidence (e.g., archeological, ethnographic, and epigraphical) are necessary to more accurately understand Indian Buddhism (see Schopen 1997).[10] Many of the concepts that scholars of religion in general and Buddhism in particular have considered fundamental are a direct result of the emphasis upon textual materials over other material culture (i.e. archaeology, epigraphy) and ethnographic descriptions.[11] Here Bailey and Mabbett illustrate this important point:

---

[10] See Schopen's forward in (Lewis 2000, pp. ix-xi), and for an anthropological point of view on the importance on ethnographic methodologies to assist historical and archaeological reconstruction. See also Whitehouse and Martin (2004).

[11] Actually, certain texts in Buddhist traditions were (and are) so dominate they have influenced a great deal of ethnography. Anthropologist, James Laidlaw writes, "Durkheim's refutation emphasized Buddhism, which, *as he rightly said*, is not centrally concerned with deities at all....Propitiation of deities is indeed common, but *no remotely reflective Buddhist, including those*

We should seek to understand the dhamma's [teachings of the Buddha] by working from an understanding of the best evidence available. That evidence is furnished, for better or worse, by the texts. They represent the Buddhist monk as a wandering holy man, and it is this image to which we must give priority in the context of Buddhism's rise (Bailey & Mabbett 2003, p. 169) (my brackets).

The priority placed upon the *texts* in ancient India creates various problems in the study of early Buddhism, problems that not only *construct* a picture of Buddhism that separate it from the cultural *reality* on the ground but also promote the texts above other earlier evidence found in Buddhist material culture (e.g., architecture, art, and epigraphy). Schopen says that this is a key problem. Here he writes:

> When Europeans first began to study Indian Buddhism systematically there were already two bodies of data available to them, and the same is true today. There was, and is, a large body of archaeological and epigraphical material, material that can be reasonably well located in time and space, and material that is largely unedited and much of which was never intended to be "read." This material records or reflects at least part of what Buddhists—both lay people and monks—actually practiced and believed. There was, and is, an equally large body of literary material that in most cases cannot actually be dated and that survives only in very recent manuscript traditions. It has been heavily edited, it is considered canonical or sacred, and it was intended—at the very least—to inculcate an ideal. The material records what a small, atypical part of the Buddhist community wanted that community to believe or practice. Both bodies of material, it is important to note, became available to Western scholars more or less simultaneously. The choice of sources for the scholar interested in knowing what Indian Buddhism had been would seem obvious. But the choice made was, apparently, not based on the assessment of the two kinds of sources as historical witnesses, but on some other kind of assumption. This assumption, it appears, more than anything else has determined the status and use of archaeological and epigraphical sources in the study of Indian Buddhism, and this assumption, apparently, accounts for the fact that an overriding textual orientation was in place very early in Buddhist studies. (Schopen 1997, pp. 1–2)

This is a particularly important point especially in light of the readily apparent disparity between doctrinal prescriptions and actual behavior on the ground.

---

who spend time and resources participating in such rites, would confuse them for a moment with following the teachings of the Buddha" (2007, p. 220–21) (my italics).

Summary

In the last chapter, I argued that the ritualized disposal of dead bodies was a widespread feature of *Homo sapiens* (and possibly Neanderthal) behavior. Evidence from material culture and historical texts suggested that as human culture became more complex, professional religious guilds utilized pre-existing ritualized/compulsive behaviors and turned them into coherent "scripts" of meaning. These ritual scripts promoted lasting and powerful representations that were widely distributed throughout each distinctive culture.

The control over a widespread and recurrent feature of human behavior by religious experts highlighted the need for humans to find meaning in the face of extinction of individuals by groups. By proposing that ritualized disposal was a widespread feature of human behavior, I claimed that even Buddhist participants—who explicitly and doctrinally rejected the importance of dead bodies and the superhuman agency of dead agents—still cognitively operated on counterintuitive assumptions toward dead bodies resulting in ritualized compulsions to handle them with care.

In this chapter, I present the problem of doctrinal authority in "early" Buddhism from which handling and representing dead bodies is constrained by textual regulations reaching back to the "historical" Buddha himself. Although the evidence precludes scholars from connecting these texts to the historical Buddha by centuries or more, almost every tradition, including modern scholarship on early Buddhism, promotes the idea that the historical Buddha and the early monastic communities reject the importance of corpse disposal. The reliance on textual evidence over other types of material evidence is, in relation to Western, Victorian, and Protestant scholarship that privilege these texts as "sacred," based upon the paradigm of Christianity, the Bible, and the new field of comparative religion. On the one hand the doctrinal tradition (specifically found in texts) and monastic communities' rejection of superhuman agency are explained explicitly by religious experts as "superstitious" behavior(s) by the laity. However, on the other hand, religious and ritualized behavior toward dead bodies is promoted in almost every facet of monastic life, and the earliest material evidence supports this argument.

Part Two
BUDDHALOGICAL INCORRECTNESS

Chapter Three

Lies, Damn Lies, and Buddhist Texts

O f course, we can't ignore the texts. They are an important resource when investigating what the experts say about corpses. The pre-eminent work on the doctrines of ancient Buddhism comes from T.W. Rhys Davids and Etienne Lamotte. Rhys Davids, writing over a century ago, states that the ancient texts of Buddhism (here he is referring to the extant Pāli tradition) say nothing about the disposal of dead bodies in ancient Buddhism (see also Rhys Davids 1900; see Schopen 1997, p. 8).[1] In fact, as previously stated, there is nary a hint of any regulations concerning dead bodies in the Pāli *Vinaya* itself. If one only took the texts into consideration, one might very well conclude that behaviors neglecting dead bodies were as a matter of fact the ideological norm and Buddhists just let them die where they lay. This, of course, would seem almost impossible to believe since *most* normal individuals and communities do not allow this kind of behavior.

In his historical survey of ancient Indian Buddhism, Monsignor Lamotte (1988) claimed that while ancient Buddhist doctrines were silent about disposal of corpses, especially in the early *Vinayas* (Skt: monastic codes), *the rituals actually performed seem to be the result of a compromise between the monastic community and the laity* (see also, Decaroli 2004). In other words, such actions are categorized by some scholars as "folk" religion, not proper Buddhism (see Gomez 1987, p. 363; Swearer 1987, pp. 374-78). Stanley Tambiah (1970) ar-

---

[1] Although, as I have presented earlier, the Pāli *Vinaya* clearly states certain activities are to be preformed to the Buddha's body and relics. Interestingly enough by the time of Buddhaghoṣa's commentary (Pāli: *Visuddhimagga*) in the fifth century CE, Buddhist participants were engaging in ritual meditation of corpses (Buddhaghoṣa 1964, p. 193; Klima 2002, p. 188). This is important because Buddhaghoṣa's commentary is regularly regarded as the major representative summary of the extant Pāli tradition (Akira 1990, p. 125).

gued forcefully that such constructions of "pure" Buddhism and "folk" religion are sheer "academic" and "Western" paradigms created by scholars (see
Silk 1994; see Strong 2004). James Laidlaw writes:

> Virtually all the ethnographical description we have of Theravada Buddhism
> has emphasized how intimately interconnected the doctrinal tradition was
> and remains, in practice with local cults. David Gellner (2001) has usefully
> summarized recent anthropological work along these lines. Some authors,
> such as Tambiah have insisted that the distinction between the two is wholly
> artificial–that they can only be understood as a part of a single complex
> whole. (Laidlaw 2004, p. 94)

Actually these types of arguments, as Tambiah and I suggest, may be more
misleading than anything since we find the same types of religious activities in
the lay community as within the monastic traditions. In as much as many
scholars would like to make the distinction between monastic and lay traditions, this taxonomy appears on the surface too brittle for any real meaningful
discourse. The epigraphy, *vinayas*, and philosophical texts of monastic communities seem to indicate that monastic communities were involved in many
of the religious behaviors of their lay counterparts. Robert DeCaroli summa-
rizes the point by saying:

> Rather than simply dismiss these spirit religions as reluctant concessions to
> the masses, however, it is essential that we try to understand them and the
> nature of the beings upon which they focus. Although the two authors just
> quoted do excellent jobs of exploring aspects of these spirit-deities, my main
> objection to the positions embedded in their texts is that they deny the pos-
> sibility that these spirit-deities were important to the literate, the elite, and
> the saṃgha (the Buddhist community) itself. By setting up a dialectic between
> the monastic community and the spirit-deities, this position runs the risk of
> viewing the saṃgha as clever manipulators playing the public for the sake of
> greater donations. I believe that such a view greatly oversimplifies the process
> and fails to recognize that the monks and nuns themselves were participants
> in the culture around them. (Decaroli 2004, p. 10)

Bones, Stones, and Schopen's Monks

Gregory Schopen has argued at great length that the evidence does not support the claim that monastic Buddhists were involved in non-religious behav-

ior. In fact, epigraphy seems to indicate that monks were involved in all sorts of social behavior including, accumulating wealth, paying votive offerings to Buddha and other Buddhist saints, worshipping *stūpas* and texts, and teaching these practices to the laity (N. A. Falk 1989, pp. 156–57; Schopen 1997). Here the authors of the *Mūlasarvāstivāda-vinaya* say:

> A monk who dwells in a cemetery, robing himself with burial cloth, must not enter a monastery. He must not worship a *stūpa*. If he should worship, he must not approach it any nearer than a fathom. He must not use a monastic cell [sleeping quarters]. He must not even sit on monastic bedding. He must not sit among the community of monks. He must not teach Dharma to Brahmans and householders [lay people] who have come and assembled. He must not go to the houses of Brahmans and householders, and so on. (Schopen 1995, p. 474) (my brackets)

This passage affirms that there were different categories within the monastic community (cemetery monks and non-cemetery monks). More importantly, the passage shows regulations made concerning activities of monks who inhabited these cemeteries. This raises some very interesting questions. First, why would the monastic community not want these cemetery monks to interact with others in the monastic community? Second, why would they not want these *special* monks to "worship" *stūpas*, to commute outside the monastic complex, or at least the cemetery, and to sit inside the monastic cells within the *vihāra* (Skt: monastery)? These questions might be answered by an interesting comment by Paul Harrison. Here he says:

> The followers of the *Bodhisattva* [Mahayana] way clearly had to face the fact that, despite all their polemic and hyperbole, they shared their membership of the *sangha* [monastic community] with people who continued to believe that arhatship [non-Mahayana] was the ultimate goal of Buddhist practice. (Harrison 1987, p. 83) (my brackets)

I would argue that the first question is therefore answered because the cemetery monks were doing exactly what the prohibitions of the *Mūlasarvāstivāda-vinaya* stated. *Vinaya* rules were usually created *post hoc* in nature to problems that confronted the monastic community (see Corless 1990, p. 104; Williams 1989, p. 4-6; Williams & Tribe 2002, pp. 99–104).

The Myth of the Mahāyāna

The textual evidence seems to imply that the cemetery monks were teaching certain things to members of the monastic community, teachings that the elder community didn't approve of, and they were teaching these same things to the laity.[2] In addition, the kinds of activities that Buddhist scholars associate with the Mahāyāna movement (i.e., belief in *śūnyatā* [Skt: emptiness]; worshiping of *stūpas*, relics, spirits, ghosts, and *buddhas*; the production, recitation, and copying of books that then were worshiped in *stūpas*; and then the teaching that anyone lay or monastic could achieve liberation by a path known as the *bodhisattva* ideal [Akira 1990, p. 270]) occur in sectarian communities as well.[3]

Actually, the Mahāyānists who "lived" within the monastic complex probably were the ones that created and copied the polemical texts that we categorize presently as Mahāyāna. Being a Mahāyānist, or differing in philosophical position from the goal of *arhantship* (Skt: *arhat*, i.e., one who has attained enlightenment in the monastic order by help of the Buddha and his teaching), did not preclude being a member of the *Saṃgha*/Sangha (Skt: monastic community), since inclusion into the order was based upon taking *Vinaya* proscriptions (Williams & Tribe 2002, pp. 97, 100-2). Schopen observes,

---

[2] Teaching is probably too soft a categorization of this activity. In fact, if the Pāli *Vinaya* is any indication of the type of proselytizing going on by cemetery monks, then the *Vinaya*'s description of the Buddha and his close followers appears quite zealous in their missionary activities of conversion. Sometimes even using fear in the process of conversion (see Brekke 2002, pp. 26, 32, 88-90). They weren't passive missionaries; more so, they were in all probability very active Buddhist evangelicals. This view may conform to the Paul Harrison's argument that at least one of the origins of the Mahāyāna was a fundamentalist ascetic reaction to monastic Buddhists (1995, p. 65).

[3] In fact there are a growing number of scholars (including myself) who reject a single colossal movement such as the Mahāyāna (e.g., Paul Williams, Paul Harrison, Jonathan Silk, and Gregory Schopen). Here Schopen says, "Surely we are now beyond talking about '*the* Mahāyāna" as if it were a single, monolithic thing, beyond using that very designation as anything other than a heuristic device...we are also well beyond, looking for a single causes for the emergence or 'rise' of what is clearly not a single thing" (Schopen 2005, pp. 94-95). What we now call Mahāyāna was a combination of different beliefs and behaviors in ancient India that resulted in largely marginal movement up until and not earlier than the fifth/sixth century CE and probably more likely the seventh century and later in India (Schopen 2005, pp. 14-17).

that out of the earliest (eighty) inscriptions that "appear to be Mahāyāna," seventy percent are donations from the monastic community, a mere twenty percent are from the laity (Schopen 1997, p. 31). Therefore, early material evidence supports that Mahāyāna Buddhists were from the monastic community or supported by the monastic community.

To view South Asian Buddhism with Chinese eyes

By the seventh century of the Common Era, the well-known Chinese pilgrim Hsüan-tsang commented that in ancient Gayā "all Mahāyānists of the Sthavira [Skt.; Pāli: Theravāda] School, all [were] perfect in Vinaya observances." (Dutt 2000, p. 175; see also Beal 2004, ii, p. 133) (my brackets). In addition, Sukumar Dutt (2000) comments that "there is no 'Sthavira School' in Mahāyāna Buddhism, and Hsüan-tsang's commentary must have meant that all the monks he refers to were of Mahāyānist faith and yet were particular about the observance of *Vinaya* rules as the monks of the Theravāda school" (p. 175). However, put in the context of Williams' (also Harrison's and Schopen's) argument, Hsüan-tsang probably did see Mahāyānists observing the sectarian *Vinaya* rules of the monastic complexes in Gayā and elsewhere (e.g., Udyāna, Ceylon). They differed on theoretical matters, yet were Buddhists by the same *Vinaya*.[4] Many of the stereotypes of the monks of early Buddhism (e.g., wandering ascetic, separated by theoretical concerns) appear to be strangely irregular from the norm taken from the earliest material and textual evidence.[5]

In fact, many of the idealized forest, begging monk roles and behaviors appear not to be the case according to the evidence. Here the *Mūlasarvāstivāda-vinaya* states:

---

[4] According to Steven Collins (1990), the Pāli Theravāda tradition came to prominence during disputes between rival sectarian Buddhist communities in ancient Ceylon (modern Sri Lanka), specifically the Mahavihara/Abhayagiri rivalry. The Mahaviharas apparently won the favor and support of the ruling elite at the time and became the sect representing "original" Buddhism in Ceylon. "[A]t certain periods Abhayagiri was clearly the more numerous and dominant [than the Mahaviharas]. It seems that at least from the 3rd century A.D., and perhaps before, the Abhayagiri used what we would now call Mahayana texts" (p. 96) (my brackets).

[5] However, the evidence of the Chinese writer I Ching (seventh century CE) seems to argue that nuns in ancient (actually middle/late) Indian Buddhism were participating in these types of behavior (e.g., begging, ascetic, and impoverished) in the monastic and lay environment (N. A. Falk 1989, p. 157).

At that time in Sravasti there was a householder named Sresthin who was rich... He took a wife from a similar family...but when there was neither son nor daughter...the househoulder became pious in regard to the Blessed One [The Buddha]. Eventually he approached a monk: "Noble One," he said, "I wish to enter the order of this well spoken dharma and *Vinaya*." "Do so, good sir," said the monk and in due order, after shaving the house holder's head, he began to give him the rules of training. But the householder was overcome with a serious fever that created an obstacle to his entering the order.

The monks reported this matter to the Blessed One. The Blessed One said: "He must be attended to, but the rules of training are not to be given until he is again healthy." (Schopen 1995, p. 498) (my brackets)

So, cemetery monks were engaged in teaching individuals in the monastic community who in all probability produced what are considered Mahāyāna texts (e.g., *prajñāpāramitā* literature), and they also taught the laity many of the superhuman aspects associated with the lay Mahāyāna movement.[6] The laity obliged this teaching. And why not, the cemetery monks had inside knowledge; *they controlled the important rituals of death.*

Ghosts, Buddhist Gods, and Globalization

Robert Decaroli (2004) has recently argued convincingly that the early Indian Buddhist Saṃgha utilized a full range of religious repertoire, including the association with "spirit-deities" and funeral customs that predate Buddhism. In some cases, the Buddhist Saṃgha performed ritualized actions to alleviate a spiritual/religious vacuum that existed with regard to salient notions concerning hungry ghosts (Skt: *preta*) or "spirit-deities" (e.g., *rākṣasas, gandharvas, piśā-cas, yakṣas,* and *nāgas*) and incorporated established religious systems into the developing community. In addition, the monastic complexes were located in special places (Skt: *caitya*), many times near/on cemeteries or charnel grounds that the mainstream Indian population and the Saṃgha recognized as religious in nature because these *special* locations predate Buddhism. Finally, this inclusiveness towards older religious systems and salient disposal customs allowed

---

[6] I have given numerous papers on these interesting behaviors in conferences starting in the spring of 1997 at the Mid-West *American Academy of Religion* (Terre Haught, IN), resulting in several papers submitted for publication in 2009–2010.

the growing monastic community to attract a plethora of religious and economic patrons (e.g., elite, lay, and monastic) to sustain and further the growth of Indian Buddhism as a whole.

The argument that the Buddhist *Saṃgha* utilized pre-existing burial locations and performed religious ritualized actions in direct concert with these locations is important to this thesis because it illustrates that monastic Buddhists were involved in certain behaviors outside the characterization "pristine" Buddhism (e.g., forest ascetic, non-supernatural ideals or behaviors, not disposing of dead bodies by means of ritualized actions). Schopen, once again illustrates:

> Much has been written recently about modern Buddhist "forest monks" and the Pāli *Vinaya* also speaks of such Monks. But in one passage of this monastic code in which the life style of such monks is most clearly described there are, again, some surprises.

> These passages from several different *vinayas*—and a large number of other passages—make it difficult to avoid the conclusion that if the ideal of the individual rag-wearing, begging, forest-dwelling monk was in fact ever the rule in the early history of Indian Buddhism, if the ideal was ever anything more than "emblematic," then it was, by the time the *vinayas* that we have were compiled, all but a dead letter. (Schopen 1995, p. 475; also published in Schopen 2004, p. 93)

The Histories of Buddhism

Schopen also notes the *post hoc* character of texts in early Buddhism concerning death rituals. While the Pāli tradition is silent on this matter a parallel, or rival, *Mūlasarvāstivāda-vinaya* text is not. In the *Mūlasarvāstivāda-vinaya*, doctrines dictating the procedures for disposal were generated after the Hindu laity became upset over Buddhist corpses being left out in the middle of the road (Schopen 1997, p. 217).

If monastic codes were a reaction to a problem that faced the Buddhist community, then it is not surprising; therefore, that in the *Mūlasarvāstivāda-vinaya* procedures for the ritual disposal of the dead bodies of monks were generated to appease the laity (Decaroli 2004; see also, Lopez Jr. 1995;

Schopen 1997, p. 218), though this historical account more than smells of a *post hoc* explanation for naturally occurring human behavior towards corpses.[7]

Summary

Texts played a significant role in the development of Buddhist traditions. In fact, scholars have utilized texts over other types of evidence in their formulations about early Buddhism and the historical development of the various Buddhist traditions throughout Asia. In Chapter Three, I traced the doctrinal authority of corpse disposal and regulations from various sectarian monastic codes and commentary. Western scholars, driven by ideological and cultural biases on selecting certain texts over other types of important evidence, stressed the significance of one such important text (i.e., the Pāli *Vinaya*). In doing so, scholars raised the authority of the Pāli tradition as representative of early Buddhism.

The Pāli tradition, found throughout Sri Lanka (Ceylon) and Southeast Asia (known as **Theravāda**), historically has claimed authority over other Buddhist traditions on the earliest doctrinal matters. In the Pāli tradition, there was almost no reference to regulations concerning corpse disposal, suggesting considerable redaction in comparison to parallel traditions. However, closer investigation demonstrated that explicit rules were added by the monastic community to appease the laity; although, it is not entirely clear what the stance of the community was prior to these new rules.

Some of these regulations appeared to circumvent powerful counterintuitive representations (e.g., hauntings, improper handling) concerning the dead to the lay community. The attention to special handling of the dead, internment in burial mounds, and relic worship—many of which likely predate Buddhism—created specialized experts (e.g., cemetery monks) who may have

---

[7] I do not question the fact that it may have happened to the **Mūlasarvāstivādin** community; however, as my argument in Chapter One states, the majority of humans (including Buddhists) simply don't behave this way in regard to dead bodies on a normal basis. The chances of this behavior occurring outside of an atypical occurrence were highly unlikely in mainstream Buddhist society. Though a historical problem in this example and not part of my larger argument, I would suggest that the behaviors or rules (oral or written) concerning dead bodies in the *Mūlsarvāstivāda-vinaya* were probably in place long before the explanation for the rule.

challenged the authority of the conventional Buddhists in the monastic complexes by seizing upon ritualized compulsions to corpses that provided "meaningful" scripts of ritual and doctrine to the laity.

Many scholars have argued that Buddhist texts re-enforce a division between the laity and monastic community on matters of ritual disposal; however, the texts themselves revealed that monastic Buddhists were involved in myriad ritual (scripted) behaviors towards dead agents. Epigraphical donative inscriptions reveal that monastic Buddhists gained a great deal of wealth by performing special actions to dead agents for the laity. Many of these donations were also made by monastic Buddhists themselves. Although some scholars charged this counterintuitive behavior to the rise of a later movement known as the Mahāyāna, the textual and material evidence implied that this was the practice of mainstream sectarian Buddhism throughout South Asia.

It seems that monastic believers were not only involved in mortuary behavior from a very early period, but many of these behaviors coincided with an abundant repertoire of ritual actions that gave the early (or sectarian) Buddhist monastic communities widespread appeal, wealth, and socio-political power in ancient India. Moreover, I argued, that Buddhist texts reveal that specific attention to mortuary behavior may have filled a "religious" vacuum that existed in regard to counterintuitive inferences that greatly concerned the laity concerning dead agents.

Chapter Four

Stupa, Relic, and Hungry Ghost

The proscriptions of the writers in the *Mūlasarvāstivāda-vinaya* make explicit claims about what to do when a monk dies. First, a gong is to be sounded to alert the Buddhist community as a whole. Second, the body of the deceased was to be taken from the place of death to the cemetery by the monks entitled to the dead monk's belongings. Third, a cremation ceremony was enacted by special cemetery monks. Fourth, the inheritors of the dead monk's estate (alms bowl, belongings etc.) performed ritual circumambulation around a *stūpa* that contained relics of the Buddha or other relics of special Buddhist agents. Fifth, a dharma sermon was read aloud to the community still present (Schopen 1997, p. 208). As noted earlier, other proscriptions were made against cemetery monks in the *Mūlasarvāstivāda-vinaya* from participating in the circumambulation of the *stūpa* (Schopen 1995, p. 474).

As a result the cemetery monks were not entitled to the belongings of the dead monk since they were not participants in the end of the ritual itself. It is also important to note that there is no mention of where the cremated remains of the dead monk were or if they (cemetery monks) were present for the circumambulation and the dharma reading as well. The question remains; what part of the ritual dealt with the dead body and why does the *Mūlasarvāstivāda-vinaya* text not mention the body in the remainder of the ritual itself?[1]

---

[1] Schopen raises an important series of cases where some dead Buddhist monks simply were cremated and their remains were left in the funeral yard without the building of a *stūpa* for their remains. Of course, this resulted in "hauntings" by dead monks towards monks who had taken possession of the deceaseds' properties (Schopen 1997, p. 104). Therefore, not all monks were placed into ritually erected *stūpa* and were the recipients of relic worship. In addition, it

When One Burial Simply Will Not Do

Robert Hertz (1960) offers a particularly insightful theory that might explain our Buddhist case study. Hertz argues that in many cultures a "twice burial" occurs. The first burial symbolizes the biological problem death represents to society. A dead body is the inevitable fact of human life. It also represents a very dangerous possibility for the community at large, since the stability or failure of a community's survival might depend upon this person, now dead, especially in *l' environnement antique.*

In the first burial, the gong that is sounded and the cremation ceremony in the *Mūlasarvāstivāda-vinaya* explicitly highlight Hertz's theory that this was very important to the community and its survival. The body is made a source of biological pollution in many cultures in the first burial, the reason being that the body is a symbol for the potential collapse of the social unit (it is dangerous). In addition, many times the body is used in special actions (rituals) that bring the body to be purified (by fire, smoke, water, blood, or other purifying agents),[2] or specifically treated (beaten, shaken, touched, kissed, spit upon, or treated in a horrifying manner) to reinforce the apparent biological danger a dead body presents to the community.

Those who come into contact with the body during this stage are usually considered to be contaminated by the polluted body. These are usually the family of the deceased or the entire village or group. They may either purify themselves through other ritual activities including ritual washing, or some may live as contagious *ad infinitum* as in the case of the cemetery monks of the *Mūlasarvāstivāda-vinaya* (seen earlier as prohibited from contact with various *vihāra* monks, Brahmins, and the laity).[3]

The *second* burial in Hertz's twofold system has very little to do with the body itself. In fact, the second burial, which may happen shortly thereafter,

---

appears there are three separate types of disposal (e.g., funeral rites (*śarīra-pūjā*), internment at a *stūpa*, and relic veneration by a cult) in place.

[2] Notice blood is sometimes used. The handling of bodily fluids such as blood is quite dangerous and many diseases (e.g., HIV, Hepatitis) are spread through human contact with blood and other bodily fluids.

[3] For a Cantonese version of corpse handlers that are "permanently contaminated" see J. L. Watson (1982, p. 170).

weeks later, or years later, involves the redistribution of the dead person's material resources and re-integration of the deceased's social roles in the community. The biological danger has been recognized by the community in the first burial, exposing the "fragility" of the social organism (R. S. Watson 1988c, p. 203), and now the community has re-distributed and re-organized to show that society conquers biology (Bloch & Parry 1982, p. 5). Society then becomes transcendent from ancestral times and conquers the limits (death) of individual participation within the social organism (Bloch & Parry 1982, p. 15; see also Eliade 1965).

This may explain the problem concerning the explicit lack of information on the cremains in the *Mūlasarvāstivāda-vinaya*.[4] The regulation explicitly stated in the text is important in the *Vinaya* only because it applies to the danger to the community, since monastic codes are for the protection of living members of the *Saṃgha*. The cremation is performed by the cemetery monks and the monks entitled to the dead monk's possessions. The non-cemetery monks proceed through the remainder of the ritual. They must, as noted earlier, "wash themselves" and "change their dress" (Schopen 1997, p. 314; 2004, p. 218; J. L. Watson 1982, p. 168). Nevertheless, after the cremation, the body/cremains are not important for the community's survival, although the dry relics are used in further ritual activity to promote Buddhist religiosity. The monks who have cared for the person (now dead) continue participating in the second part of the burial, which represents the re-distribution of Hertz's theory.

Hertz's theory is more than pronounced in the Mūlasarvāstivādin example. Other prohibitions in that same *Vinaya* (stated earlier) prohibit the cemetery monks from a series of actions outside of their role as cremation experts. As a matter of course, it makes good sense to think that the cemetery monks remain more than a source of pollution, since they do not participate in the second part of the disposal during which they are prohibited from teaching

---

[4] This isn't a problem peculiar to the **Mūlasarvāstivādins** either. After my father passed away in the middle of this research, I read in various media reports and was told that many people in the US regularly have a loved one cremated and then many times forget about their cremains for a lengthy period of time, or put off indefinitely any other secondary disposal. However, their social roles (job, family, friends; material resources; and possessions) are re-distributed fairly soon after death.

the laity, worshipping *stūpas*, or associating with others in the monastic community.

Even more interesting is a modern ethnographic description of a Buddhist ritualized body disposal in Burma. Compare and contrast the *Mūlasarvāsti-vāda-vinaya* with this extended Burmese (Theravādin) example. Here Melford Spiro (1982) writes,

> After death, the deceased lies in a state in his own house for a minimum of three days before he is buried or cremated. This, informants claim, is to permit relatives from distant places to attend the funeral. Immediately after death the corpse is washed: typically by relatives, and always by males. *Women do not wash the corpse because, so it is claimed, they are afraid that its ghost (tasei) might harm them.* This is confusing...because many Burmese seem to be holding several notions simultaneously, all anti-Buddhist....[T]he soul may be hostile, angry, or evil, and rituals are performed to protect the family from its hostility.
>
> From the time of death until the day of the funeral, a steady stream of visitors passes through the household, and from the time of death until seven days after the funeral (the period of formal morning) the immediate family of the deceased are never alone. They are fed by relatives, who not only cook their meals but also make arrangements for the funeral, feed the guests, feast (sic) the monks, and so on.

Notice that the women in Spiro's observations do not perform ritualized actions (washing) toward the corpse because the dead body might harm them, clearly an example of the belief in counterintuitive agency given to the dead body. Moreover, the role of women has changed from the earlier historical material where women were able to ward off counterintuitive agents in the burial yard. Here Spiro goes on to say:

> [T]he monks recite the *paritta* which permanently expel the soul from the world of the living, the house and courtyard of the deceased are filled with groups of men who gamble at cards until dawn. One of these groups always plays in a room where the corpse is laid out. The explanation for this custom is that it protects the bereaved from the deceased's ghost or the fear of it. For the same reason lanterns are hung around the courtyard not only to provide light for the gamblers, but to keep the ghosts away.
>
> Although the ghost is feared, it is not ignored. Before the burial, for example, jaggery (a form of molasses) and rice are placed in a bowl at the cemetery for the ghost to eat, and when the corpse is buried the bowl is placed with the

body inside the coffin. Similarly, the day before the monks are called to recite the *paritta* which finally sends the soul to its next abode, *the spouse of the deceased calls the ghost to the house to be witness to the ceremony.*

The same special recitation is used as the nuns used earlier; however, now monks recite the *paritta*, leaving these special utterances still important but in control of the monks. Nevertheless, it is interesting that other precautionary actions are taken to bar the counterintuitive agents (ghosts) from becoming malevolent (a common theme in many cultures). What is fascinating is that these actions are meant to keep the ghosts at bay; however, they also leave out food so that the ghosts will not go away hungry. It is curious that ghosts in many cultures are hungry soon after death (and that many in the community recognize this psychological state), as many ritualized disposals include food and drink that are included in their ritualized actions. Finally Spiro writes:

> What is not explained, however, is why *women are never present at night*; or why, if the men are present to provide protection for the family, they play cards; or why, if they play cards they gamble. There is little to indicate from the demeanor of the card players that a death has occurred.

> [I]n general [they] behave in an entirely casual manner.

> There being no professional morticians or gravediggers in the village, the male relatives of the deceased dig the graves or prepare the funeral pyre. Before burial or cremation, the flowers that have been in the room with the body at home are scattered in the cemetery, symbolizing, so the villagers say, the separation of the deceased from the living. Similarly, if the body is cremated, the food for the ghost which is usually buried with the corpse is scattered in the cemetery. (pp. 248–52) (my emphasis and brackets in all passages)

The marginalized nun as an instigator for religious efficacy

The contrast between the *Mūlasarvāstivāda-vinaya* and Spiro's Burmese account are interesting. Notice that the role of the cemetery monk has been completely replaced by family members of the deceased. Decaroli notes that females were in many cases in ancient India associated with cemeteries and funeral rituals.[5] Specifically, he states that female nuns were trained in "writing" and "protective spells" (Skt: *paritta*) that gave them supernatural abilities to reside and face dangerous "cemetery dwellers" in the cemetery/charnel grounds (Decaroli 2004, p. 41). However, there are no extant nuns (Pāli: *bhikkhunīs*) in Theravāda traditions like the Burmese example. They died out in India centuries earlier (see N. A. Falk 1989). The problem of allowing nuns in Theravada traditions, such as Burma, is complicated by the fact that Pāli *Vinaya* rules exclude nuns from entering the order without another already admitted nun performing the admittance ritual (*Kullavagga* X. 17, 4–8. pp. 351–55) (cited by N. A. Falk 1989; Gross 1993; Rhys-Davids & Oldenberg 1998b, pp. 351–55; Slone & Mort 2005). Ergo, there cannot be any more nuns in the Theravāda tradition.[6]

The importance, or lack thereof, of nuns in both early/middle Indian Buddhism and modern Theravāda examples can't be ignored. If nuns were allowed to write and perform very important ritualized disposal actions in ancient India, then why did they die out in the Theravāda tradition? One explanation is that nuns in the sectarian traditions of early Indian Buddhism controlled very powerful rituals concerning death and dead spirits-deities. Their status allowed them to have important contact with the mainstream Indian community at large and possibly write their beliefs in texts.[7] So, nuns may in fact be the connection between the evangelical cemetery monks of the Mūlsarvāstivādin community previously discussed and the *vihāra* (Skt: monastic residence) monks who were prohibited from association with these individuals.

---

[5] Though apparently there were no *stūpas* dedicated to nuns; therefore, it is hardly likely that the nuns were able to build a donative cult and center around their community. Schopen maintains, "that nowhere in either the archaeological or the epigraphical records do we find an instance of *stūpa* having been built for a nun." [T]he *stūpa*...was a source of revenue and support for...fellow monks" (Schopen 2004, p. 349).

[6] Some interesting and creative possibilities have emerged that Mahāyāna nuns (since they are nuns who have taken monastic vows) could perform the ceremony for the Theravāda community; however, no such action has taken place to date (Slone & Mort 2005, pp. 5–6). Falk uses the *Bhikkhunīvibanga* for her evidence; Slone and Mort cite Falk's evidence.

[7] In fact, according to the Pāli *Vinaya*, monks were allowed to teach nuns the *Vinaya* (Rhys-Davids & Oldenberg 1998b, p. 344, Kullavagga X, 8.1).

Explicitly, the *Mūlasarvāstivāda-vinaya* states that the cemetery monks were not to share sleeping quarters (cells) or "sit" upon the bedding of the *vihāra* monks. Though the contamination of dwelling in a cemetery seems like the obvious choice, might this also be an implicit reference to monks and nuns (who were in the cemetery) engaging in procreative actions as well? The implication that monks and nuns engaged in this type of activity is not out of the question, since in the Pāli *Vinaya* there are rules that were created to penalize such behavior. In addition, the cult surrounding the worship of written texts contained within *stūpas* (usually associated with the Mahāyāna movement) may have in fact been instigated by nuns proselytizing and performing dynamic mortuary behavior to mainstream Indian communities and members of the *Saṃgha* that resided in the *vihāra*.[8]

If the nuns controlled important rituals such as those for disposing of bodies, then I suggest that the community at large (dominated by males) would have tried in various ways to subjugate these nuns to inferior roles, or, as in the Theravāda tradition, completely reduce their status to nothing, an outsider in the Buddhist monastic community.

The family, then, in the modern descriptions takes on the role of the cemetery monks/nuns in the disposal of bodies and is therefore stripped of authority within the ritual; material resources are then re-distributed to the monastic community at large. This may take the form of huge financial expenditures for the family as donors to have larger numbers of monks present at the funeral (Spiro 1982, p. 457). Notice that the monks in the Burmese account are in charge of the protective *parittas*, whereas in the early Indian example this was the role of the nuns. The Indian *bhikkhunī* and her role were then "outsourced" to family of the deceased for which they fulfilled the role of the contagious burial participants, while the *Saṃgha* gained control over the salient power of the dead person's restless spirit and their social and material resources.

---

[8] See Willis (1985, 1992) for interesting arguments on the roles of monastic nuns and donative practices by lay women in the spread of Indian Buddhism.

Selling the Dharma
(and Rolling It through Asia)

One of the central issues when considering the treatment of dead bodies is the agency of the person who has died. Most living things are agents; they can move themselves and cause other things to move.[9] Once most living things die, they are no longer considered to be agents; however, dead bodies in particular activate those cognitive inference systems involved in, among other things, agency detection. In Indian Buddhist texts there are stories of dead monks who haunt monasteries because certain rituals have not been performed on the corpse (Schopen 1997, pp. 210-13). Moreover, the early Buddhist texts are filled with stories of counterintuitive agents who haunt the living or possess them for various reasons (e.g., Decaroli 2004). After the eighth century (CE), Chinese Buddhist texts (many unfamiliar to the Indian tradition), describe those procedures necessary to handle the problem of *hungry ghosts* (Lopez Jr. 2001, pp. 174-75).

This characteristic of a dead person haunting the living is a very familiar theme in many cultures of the world. Whether it is dead ancestors, or an accidental death, or a malevolent spirit, stories are told around the world about dead people still having an effect. Since a dead body is obviously no longer an agent, why do humans consistently create stories about dead people still capable of acting? Jesse Bering writes:

> In fact, though the anecdotal database ostensibly leaves little to the imagination, there have been absolutely no controlled experimental studies done to assess how individuals *actually* represent the minds of those who have died. Atran and Norenzayan (in review) note one problem with the above model: because they are invisible, causal intuitions dealing with spirits must be realized *in absentia* of an actual agent; even the *expectation* that there exists material agency behind actions can never be realized in principle, since it is precisely the agent's supposed counterintuitive properties [invisible +PERSON] which provides it with a conceptual identity.

---

[9] It might be argued that plants are not agents and can't move things; however, the argument could be made that they are in fact agents. The fact is that most plants move very slowly and their growth and movement over time regularly involve the uprooting of the earth and sidewalks, causes power-lines to snap, and in the unique case of the Venus Flytrap (*Dionaea muscipula*) eats insects and animals.

The postulate that *ghost* is a cultural invention may be misguided in that it overlooks the possibility that not only the spontaneous inference system triggered by it, but also the very concept itself, has natural foundations in the human mind. In other words, is it possible that the general idea of an afterlife is not so much implanted in people's heads by way of "exposure" to counterintuitive tales, as it is *already present*, already firmly entrenched in representational structures endemic to human cognition, and only then conceptually enriched through cultural channels? Can we not scarcely help *but* believe in some form of psychological continuity of the dead? To answer these questions, we must look at both the evolutionary and developmental emergence of those cognitive systems necessarily involved in the formation and maintenance of afterlife beliefs, and how these systems might be instantiated upon actual encounters with death and upon reasoning about the mental status of the deceased. (Bering 2002, p. 268-69)(emphasis in original)

Bering's point is that little is known from experimental and evolutionary psychology about why and how humans attribute agency to the deceased. However, what seems to be a problem that needs to be explored in more detail is the mental processing of biological death by the activation of various mental systems and conflicting information (by these various systems) concerning the biological and psychological death of a corpse. This will be explored in chapters seven thru nine.

Relics Recapitulate Rituals

A Chinese Buddhist ritual text (again unknown in the Indian tradition) called the *Sutra for the Spell That Brought Deliverance to the Flaming Mouth Hungry Ghost* (Chin: *Fo shuo qiuba yankou egui tuoluoni jing*) details the difficulties associated with persons still acting on the world after death, as well as, those rituals needed to mitigate these difficulties (Lopez Jr. 2001, p. 173-79). In China, Korea, and Japan,[10] from the eighth century CE on, Buddhist rituals are almost exclusively for disposal of bodies and their function in terms of avoiding problems with *hungry ghosts* or any number of similar phenomena (Buswell Jr. 1992; Earhart 1992; Plath 1964; Reader 1991; Sanford et al. 1992; Smith

---

[10] In Japan ritualized disposal is dominant in the practice of modern Buddhist traditions. Ian Reader (1991) has argued that the Japanese are "born Shinto" but "die Buddhist." Others argue that the symbiotic relationship between *Shinto* and Buddhism was an inevitable occurrence because they, very simply, needed each other to exist (see Earhart 1992).

1974; Tanabe Jr. 1999; Teiser 1988; J. L. Watson & Rawski 1988b) (see *Pictures* 4.1 & 4.2).[11] The spread of Buddhism to these areas can be directly traced along the land and maritime routes of merchants throughout Asia (see *Figure* 4.1) (Williams 1989, p. 8).[12]

There is abundant archaeological evidence for the existence of burial complexes (many of them pre-existing burial grounds)[13] along these merchant routes at places like (Indian sites) Bhārhut, Sāñchī, Amarāvatī, Nāgārjunakoṇḍa, Gandhar (modern Afganistan), Kokebe (Sri Lanka), Nigālī (Nepal) etc. (Conze 1980; Harle 1994; Lamotte 1988; Schopen 1997, 2004, pp. 360–61, 373–74).

The great Buddhist king of Ancient India, Aśoka, built elaborate monuments commemorating the relationship between Buddhism, the afterlife and the meaning of death (e.g., rock edicts XIII, IX, I, V).[14] These findings support the claim that ritualized disposal played a significant role in Buddhism from its origins to modern times. Relics from these rituals were an exceedingly "effective means" by which Buddhism spread "into areas where it had previously not existed" (Strong 2004, p. 231).[15]

---

[11] See Herman Ooms' (1975) summary of Smith's Ancestor worship.

[12] I am not suggesting that every mortuary complex was involved in long-distance trade. In fact, Fogelin (2006), using evidence from Thotlakonda (a monastic/mortuary complex in ancient Eastern India), suggests that some sites were involved in trade, money lending, and donative cults with the localized laity, rather than extensive long-distance trade (pp. 147–48, 167–68, 193–94, and 195–201).

[13] In fact, the oldest known Buddhist *stūpa*, that can be dated pre-Aśokan, contained animal, not human, remains inside them (Schopen 2004, p. 373). This may make the case that either Buddhists participated in older ritual behavior, or as Schopen has coined behavior, around the "proto-historical dead" (p. 374). Also, as Decaroli adds, "the early Buddhist community seems to have, with great regularity, positioned their religious centers directly over sites associated with funerary practices" (2004, p. 44).

[14] See Nikam & McKeon 1959. One of the peculiar features of Aśoka's "rock edicts" is that they appear in a Western trading language and script (e.g., *Brāhmī*), that very few if any local inhabitants probably could read or understand. Aśoka may have had recitations from designated oral experts. However, could anyone understand the edicts, if they were in this language and script? See additionally Dutt 2000, p. 117.

[15] See also Germano & Trainer 2004; Swearer 2004; Trainer 2006.

Picture 4.1 Monument to the Korean Victims of World War II (Hiroshima)

Picture 4.2 360° Hologram Monument to Ground Zero Victims(Hiroshima)

The Spread of Buddhism

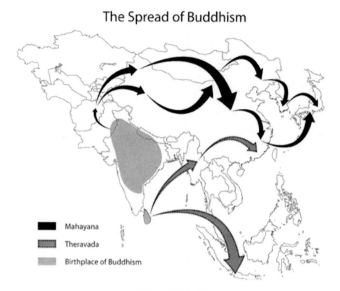

Figure 4.1 Buddhist Migration

Summary

In Chapter Four, I claimed that another important sectarian text in Buddhism—marginalized until recently—gave extremely precise rules and regulations for mortuary behavior. In it great care was taken to demarcate cemetery monks from the monastery and monastic community, and the apparent pollution in regard to the fresh corpse and any contagion associated with the dead body. The division of both special people and between clean/polluted spatial areas suggested that extensive rules were in place to limit the authority of the cemetery specialists and, also, control the powerful representations and behaviors associated with the dead.

In fact, following the theory of Robert Hertz's "Twice Burial," this sectarian Buddhist community offered specific rules for the fresh corpse as a biological danger to the community and the secondary treatment of redistributing a dead agent's social persona, roles, and material possessions back into the Buddhist community. I argued that this "twice burial" revealed a power struggle between the orthodox Buddhist leadership and the growing religious influence of the cemetery specialists; in addition, "twice burial" reflected concern toward the growing attention for stability of the monastic group.

By drawing on comparative mortuary behavior between a sectarian monastic code and more recent ethnography in Burma, I claimed that many of the cemetery specialists may have been female nuns, trained in both the monastic doctrines and specialized mortuary rites (e.g., spells) to handle dead agents and corpse disposal. Although Buddhist nuns were often marginalized according to sectarian texts, in some modern cultures they have been entirely replaced by other mortuary specialists, or the family of the deceased. I theorized that nuns may have occupied an extremely powerful ritual position in sectarian Buddhist traditions; therefore, putting them at odds with the orthodox leadership in the monastic community. Slowly over time, the leadership of these communities may have become fearful of the growing religious significance of the nuns and the attraction of the laity to them.

The spread of Buddhist traditions appears to have been successful due to both the attention to ritual disposal of dead bodies and the convergence of trade on the merchant routes where monastic complexes were built and occupied in proximity to (often pre-existing) cemeteries and charnel grounds. Moreover, actions involving the remains of dead bodies—relics—encouraged more ritual behavior in addition to the special disposal of dead bodies. Relics then became a salient tool to spread Buddhism throughout greater Asia, including the building of architectural monuments and monastic complexes that supported relic worship, ritual disposal of corpses, and interaction with the lay community. Relics, like texts and rituals themselves, became a viable material tool to constrain normal counterintuitive beliefs and ritualized behaviors into a distinctive Buddhist vocabulary and discourse.

Chapter Five

The Domestication of Living Buddhist Traditions

T he literature on Buddhist ritualized disposal of dead bodies is not limited to historical texts and material artifacts. The ethnographic record is also very informative. Stanley Tambiah (1970, 1976) claims that most Buddhist traditions form their practice and texts around a historical context. This behavior is explicitly revealed by Tambiah's ethnography of Thai ascetic forest monks, where Buddhists attempted to "get back" to "original" Buddhism (Tambiah 1984). Todd Lewis (2000) claims that this behavior takes the form of the "domestication of the text," where participants attempt to bridge historical texts with present (e.g., synchronic) meanings (pp. 2–7), and also, modern beliefs and practices are sometimes based in ideal notions of past events (i.e., "original" Buddhism, Christianity, and Islam). Texts are then the bridge between Buddhist traditions of the past and beliefs and cultural contexts of the present world. Furthermore, Tambiah and Lewis, both anthropologists, argue that Buddhist traditions place their texts, practices, and identities within the historical context of the "perceived" religion, Buddhism.

On the one hand, Tambiah describes this "textual domestication" by an ascetic movement of Thai Buddhists toward idealistic notions of "pure Buddhism." On the other hand, Lewis describes the enculturation of historically (but not culturally) marginalized texts by the majority of Newar (Nepali) "normative" Buddhists and by extension other historical and cultural Buddhist traditions. Tambiah and Lewis' arguments reach at the very heart of behaviors that are associated with texts (here a text may mean an artifact or an action). This inevitably includes notions about death and the handling of dead bodies, possibly explaining why mention of ritualized disposal is nonexistent in the Pāli *Vinaya*, but so pronounced in other materials.

Tambiah (1970) traces the relationship between Thai Buddhist ritual systems and Thai Buddhists' understanding of their own connection within the broader Buddhist historical and literary tradition, evident in a fundamentalist movement of specific Thai Buddhists attempting to reconstruct from textual "ideal types" (in early Buddhism) and their identities as "wandering forest monks" (Tambiah 1970, pp. 370-77; Tambiah 1976, pp. 528-30).[1] According to Schopen's analysis of Sanskrit, Tibetan, and Pāli texts, most noticeably in the *Mūlasarvāstivāda-vinaya*, by the closure of the fifth century CE there do not in fact appear to be "wandering, forest, ascetic monks" in the South Asian context outside of the redacted Pāli descriptions (Schopen 1995, p. 475). Therefore, Tambiah's Thai forest monks are reacting towards modern Buddhism to recreate a Buddhist tradition that seemingly never existed outside of idealized textual sources.[2]

Spiro's work on the Buddhists of Burmese culture (a Theravādin tradition) highlights the problem in relation to scholarship towards the extant Pāli tradition, since even he (an anthropologist) refers to Theravādin Buddhism as "atheistic" and categorizes the Burmese into different strands of idealized Buddhist taxonomies (e.g., "Nibbanic, Kammatic, Apotropaic, and Esoteric") (Spiro 1982, p. 9-12). Moreover, Thai forest groups appear to have been *created* in Tambiah's description as *post hoc* groups in response to historical (textual) Buddhism (Tambiah 1984, pp. 53, 69, 77). Finally, present Buddhist groups, regardless of present doctrinal systems, rely on what they take to be historically accurate notions of "authentic" Buddhism (see concerning "revivals" in modern Buddhism especially, Gomez 1987, pp. 381-82). They act ac-

---

[1] Richard Gombrich has identified at least six different ways the modern Buddhist Saṃgha in Ceylon (Sri Lanka), differ from "pristine" Buddhism, such as: the ownership and inheritance of property, division by caste within the Saṃgha, the "disappearance of alms," "entry into politics," and "employment of monks in salaried positions"(Gombrich 1971, p. 294). However, as highlighted earlier many of these (probably all) behaviors, roles, and identities were already in place in ancient Buddhism, or at least by the time the "idealized texts" that we have today were collected (fifth century). See specifically Schopen (1995, 1997, 2004, 2005).

[2] In fact, Tambiah's description of one such complex in Thailand details membership of the group at *Wat Pā Bān Tat* by a *majority of Westerners led by Thai ascetic renouncers* (Tambiah 1984, pp. 142-45).

cordingly by emulating these ideas about a "pristine" Buddhism that may never have existed, ideas that Chinese redactors, Sri Lankan nationalist, and Victorian scholars help propagate (Lamotte 1983-84, pp. 4-15; Schopen 1997, 2000, pp. 1-25, 2004; Silk, 1994).

Todd Lewis makes the case that "domestication... is the dialectical historical process by which a religious tradition is adapted to a region or ethnic group's socioeconomic and cultural life" (2000, pp. 3-4).[3] Therefore, texts are best understood in relation to their "cultural history" not as pure, ideological entities (e.g., philosophical texts written by small number of elites) (pp. 166-73). Lewis, describing the uses of Newari ritual texts and popular narrative, argues that mainstream Buddhism is revealed within reciprocity of public representations (beliefs and behaviors) that shape the text as much as the text shapes the community (pp. 2-7). Therefore, the hermeneutics of culture are revealed by the texts in regard to the community that shapes them. In addition, the majority of "sources" scholars use to recreate early Buddhism (and other world religions), are based upon inherent historical problems that lend themselves to peculiar results.

Schopen (2005) maintains this was probably the case in the third to seventh century CE in China, where the Mahāyāna (which had found favor among the Chinese literati) was projected back on the Indian culture. Consequently, the Mahāyāna was perceived by "Western" scholars as a large mainstream movement in the third to seventh century Indian depiction, when in fact, it was most likely extremely marginal and on the fringes of Indian society at that time (pp. 13-17).

There are at least three reasons why the cultural histories of texts are important in understanding why "pure" Buddhism has been understood as a tradition void of counterintuitive agents and religious behavior. First, Buddhist texts were primarily created, redacted, and sustained by cultural elites, rarely

---

[3] I have several friends from Malaysia that consider themselves Muslim. They refuse to eat pork (due to what they say are prohibitions in certain texts), yet they have no problem eating shellfish. I have asked Muslims from other countries about this, and all of them have responded that Muslims are not allowed to eat pork or shellfish. I deduce from this that if a certain religious community had only one main staple of animal food (protein), the chances of it being *taboo* would be almost non-existent. Ergo, the cultural and environmental selective pressures would constrain any cultural behaviors about such *taboo* behavior. See specifically for an extensive treatment of this environmental constraint theory, *Guns, Germs, and Steel* (Diamond 1995).

concerned with behavior that conflicted with their views of Buddhism. Second, texts are almost always shaped by the culture that accepts them to be authoritative, meaning that historical texts are given modern relevance. Sometimes the cultural shaping involved projecting the "current" text onto the past or to another culture that didn't hold that extraction. Third, if Schopen is correct and the Mahāyāna as a significant movement was a projection by the Chinese upon the Indian context, then the earlier evidence supports the claim that there was religious ritualized behavior towards dead bodies that predates Mahāyāna. This means that what we know as Mahāyāna was not responsible for a "watering down" of sectarian Buddhism; religious disposal of corpses simply existed before the movements known as Mahāyāna.[4]

Buddhalogical Incorrectness

Jason Slone (2004) argues that Thai Buddhism and the problems previously encountered in the historical texts are similar. According to Slone, Theravādin Thai Buddhists are given explicit, doctrinal instructions stating that the Buddha and other dead Buddhists were (and are) *not* superhuman agents (see also, Williams 1989).[5] Nevertheless Buddhist participants, who seem to understand these same doctrinal teachings, leave the *wat* (Thai: temple/monastic complex) and then pay *pūjā* (Skt: to anoint; devotional worship) to the Buddha (who is physically dead) and other special dead agents/relics at nearby "spirit-houses" for good *karma* (Skt: doing, making; fruit or action) for their family, dead ancestors, and themselves (Slone 2004, p. 78–79) (see *Picture 5.1*).

---

[4] Though I am convinced that Schopen's argument is correct in that the evidence supports Mahāyāna movements as a much later mainstream movement in India than previously thought; I am, however, confident that proto-Mahāyāna beliefs, practices, and systems (without the name and texts) were in place much earlier in India than material/historical evidence supports.

[5] This is not special to modern non-Mahāyāna groups either, from the first century BCE in Mathurā, there are images of the Buddha represented as a super-mundane character *par excellence* (Dutt 2000, p. 189).

Picture 5.1 Couple in Kyoto, Japan, Performing Pūjā at Buddhist Temple

Additionally, material evidence at ancient sites such as Sāñchī, Bhārhut, and Ajantā (among others) include—in their epigraphy (cave inscriptions documenting the life of the monastic community)—donative inscriptions made by the monks for the laity and other monastic individuals (Schopen 1995, pp. 475-98, 1997, 2004, 2005). These inscriptions served the same purpose described by Slone's Thai *pūjā* example.[6] This "theological incorrectness" is explained by Slone as on-line, cognitive mechanisms taking precedence over off-line reasoning that takes into account explicit doctrinal knowledge. The point of this is that these doctrines run counter to the way in which cognitive mechanisms tend to represent religious ideas.

---

[6] What is significant about this is that it is not a marginal example, but probably *mainstream* Buddhism. Here, I use *mainstream* Buddhism, not as Williams employs it as non-Mahāyāna, but as the culmination of monastic and lay behavior. As I have already noted, Mahāyāna and sectarian Buddhist communities were living together within the monastic complex under the same *vinaya* rules. Ergo, Williams' mainstream Buddhists need to take into account Mahāyāna, non-Mahāyāna, and lay behaviors at monastic complexes.

Discussion and Possible Conclusions
(from the History of Buddhism)

In general, the tradition of Buddhism has been hijacked by a plethora of various sources. Through the use of extended history and development, scholars operating on Western and Protestant notions on the nature of religion, Chinese pilgrims and redactors, nationalists in various cultures, and the overall tendency to raise certain texts over other types of material evidence, lead one to believe that Buddhism is not a religion in the "supernatural" sense (meaning that Buddhists believe in counterintuitive agents and perform ritualized behavior towards them). Nevertheless, these same proponents of an atheistic "pure" Buddhism simply disregard the overwhelming evidence that Buddhism is a "religious system" like other religions of the world.[7]

Some of the arguments (especially with regard to historical dating) in the above-mentioned data imply historical and textual problems that are out of the scope of the present thesis; however, it simply cannot be dismissed that all of the evidence can be eliminated due to the problems inherent in historiography. In fact, though it is incredibly difficult to prove that many of the events ever occurred at a certain exact time and in a certain exact place based upon textual and other material evidence, the composite picture of Buddhist disposal that I have presented in chapters two through five seems to imply overwhelming evidence that Buddhists were involved in special behaviors that involved the *religious* ritualized handling of dead bodies. Furthermore, their remains/cremains and relics were used in further ritual activity to spread throughout South Asia, thus gaining material wealth and support by monastic, elite, and lay followers wherever the tradition went.

The deliberate ritualized disposal of corpses, remains, and relics supported earlier *religious* behavior that incorporated Indian participants into the developing Buddhist community. The *Saṃgha* was successful not because it gained support through the ruling elite. In fact quite to the contrary, Aśoka (one of the leading proponents of donations to the early Buddhist community) is mentioned only in a single legend where he built a specific *stūpa*, that of the "Great Tope of Sāñchī" (Dutt 2000, p. 187). This, coupled with the incorpo-

---

[7] See *Buddhism without Beliefs* (Bachelor 1997) for a modern version of this idealized Buddhism.

ration of counterintuitive agent concepts whether it be ancestors, spirits, ghosts, gods, *buddhas* or other chthonic deities that predate Buddhism in India, shows that the *Saṃgha* used a wide variety of religious "repertoire" that allowed for inclusiveness towards the larger South Indian culture and not exclusiveness (e.g., other religious movements in the sixth century BCE to the Common Era) in the early spread of the religion.

The tendency to argue that there is an early, pristine, and original Buddhism simply doesn't seem to tread water. I have exposed several weaknesses to these theories. First, that the Pāli tradition and its later extant movement (i.e., **Theravāda**) are no less antagonistic towards supernatural agents and ritualized disposal of dead bodies than other traditions (sectarian or Mahāyāna). This can be explicitly found in the Pāli sources themselves. Second, that the distinction between monastic and laity behavior appears to be an artificial construct made primarily to appease western experts on religion and other disciplines concerned with religiosity. Third, that notions concerning supernatural behavior/ritualized disposal were the product of later cults resulting in what is now called the **Mahāyāna**, simply is not the case based upon the textual and material evidence. Fourth, that philosophical systems emphasizing secular ideals about Buddhism appear to be exceptionally marginal compared to mainstream Buddhist practice, yet in many of the texts that are used to hold this view much of the evidence contained within them is explicitly concerned with superhuman agents and rituals revolving around dead agents. Finally, the argument that the behavior surrounding corpses was of later invention from the Buddha and the early *Saṃgha* appears not to be historically evident from the textual and material sources.

Though it is incredibly difficult to reconstruct what we can know about the historical Buddha himself based upon the present evidence, it appears evident that the monastic and lay movements from the earliest sources considered ritualized disposal of dead bodies to be very salient. Buddhism probability benefited from this behavior and I argue that is one of the main reasons it has spread so successfully throughout greater Asia and the world. Not simply because of the social nature or inclusiveness of the Buddhist religion, but because the ritualized disposal of dead bodies in a religious context reinforced salient representations that are easily transmitted by the evolved cognitive architecture of human minds—precisely because they are memorable (*sticky*) and easily distributed throughout history and culture.

Summary

Texts are not simply historical documents that encapsulate a material portrait of past societies. In fact, texts are sometimes *used* by individuals and groups as manuals for the guidance of belief and behavior, like a moral compass that orients the world around them. In Chapter Five, I argued that historical texts found in early Buddhism were not just used by scholars to reconstruct and analyze the past. They were many times used as "living" texts by extant religious communities, like Buddhist traditions. I proposed that these *special* texts were shaped by the individuals and groups that used them in their religious practices, and therefore they should be treated as dynamic objects involved in modes of communication. Moreover, each cultural tradition "domesticated" their sacred texts for use as social tools, to which meanings were attached not hundreds or thousands of years ago, but in their present world.

When examining some of the historical texts in early Buddhism, one notes a disparity between the scholarly perception of early Buddhist practice and the actual evidence. In many ways, scholars have perpetuated the notion that early Buddhists were, ascetic, "rag-wearing," and secular types of participants. These notions were self-propagated even by some modern Buddhists themselves. Nevertheless, the textual and material evidence supports the idea that the monastic community, while heavily organized, shared many of the same beliefs and behaviors with the lay and non-Buddhist religious communities around them. Some of these very important beliefs and practices contained notions of counterintuitive agency toward dead bodies. The elaborate rituals performed to corpses and their remains suggest that the religious community of Buddhists operated on similar tacit mental processes as other humans in treating the dead in special (ritualized) ways, even though some of their doctrines may have suggested otherwise.

In analyzing these texts through anthropological methodology (e.g., ethnography), I (and others) claim that individuals operate on at least two separate mental processes. First, humans process doctrines as encyclopedic information, storing them in memory for further use. Doctrines (like math and other cultural information) are filed away and used at a later date when they are needed. Doctrines also need to be recalled from time to time, or they get lost.

Second, humans use intuitive mental processes that are not similar to the processes used to encode encyclopedic information. Many times humans are faced with dilemmas that they have never encountered. So, they need a mental process to "figure out" what to do in each circumstance. It makes sense that all combinations and permutations of possible social, cultural, and environmental scenarios could not possibly be learned in a human lifetime. Therefore, humans are continually creative thinking creatures who adjust to novel experiences.

These two different types of mental processes may explain out disparity in the historical, material, and ethnographic evidence in regard to Buddhism and the special handling of dead bodies. Though some of the doctrines of Buddhism may reject the handling of dead bodies, and many in the monastic and lay communities may accept these doctrinal representations as factual, tacit mental processes by Buddhists (and most other humans) simply do not allow them to reject handling dead bodies in special ways, nor does it stop the generation of counterintuitive representations about the dead agents themselves. Buddhists, rather, have taken these counterintuitive beliefs and behaviors (from possibly the origins of Buddhism itself) and created a special "niche" that promoted the religiosity of Buddhist traditions throughout the world. I argued that Buddhism was (and is) a socially inclusive religious tradition(s) precisely because its participants gave meaning to naturally-occurring behavior that was (and is) cognitively optimum for the human mind.

Part Three

MENTAL CULTURE

Chapter Six

When Meaning Doesn't
Matter Anymore

People devote an enormous amount of material resources (money and goods), forsake certain resources (not going to work to earn wealth), or spend a vast amount of time dedicated to performing religious ritualized behaviors. To the outside observer, it might appear that these actions provide very little benefit for the amount of time and effort expended. In economic terms, there is very little accumulation of material gain from a cost-benefit point of view. Nevertheless, it has been argued that the outside observation of such actions provides very little insight into the cause of these behaviors because of the subjective emotions, feelings, or perceptions the participant(s) might have.

Recently, Harvey Whitehouse has said, "rituals are by their very nature puzzling activities that invite *interpretation*" (Whitehouse 2004, p. 114). On a trip to Japan, I observed various rituals concerning dead spirits in what is known as the *O-bon* festival. The *O-bon* usually takes place in the month of August (though this festival occurs at various times around the world). On the last day of the festival in Kyoto, large *kanji* (Jap: Chinese characters) are burnt into the hills around the ancient capital. I met several Japanese pilgrims who had traveled from their native villages and towns to observe the burnings. I was told that the *kanji* were lit to show the restless (dead) ancestors, who were being honored by the festival, the way home to the "Western Paradise." This was an answer that I had read in text books many times during my university career. I then asked one of my informants how they knew the way to the Western Paradise when the burning *kanji* were all around us? I was told by a women in what I assumed was her late forties, that "the ancestors (Jap: *senzo*) were just smarter than us."[1] When I first asked her the reason for the *O-bon* festival, she replied (as did others that nodded their approval), that it guided the "restless ancestors" back to the "Western Paradise." This was a textbook answer. I know this because I have seen this explanation in many textbooks and monographs over the years. I expected her to give this response. I am sure either through oral or written tradition, she picked it up at some point during her life. In other words, she *learned* this information.

The second question and answer is perhaps the most telling, I observed that the burning *kanji* were almost all around us. I asked her how these spirits were able to discern which explicit signal was "West." The question itself is defective from a commonsensical standpoint. Logically it defies spatial physics and geography. It would appear that it can't be answered by regular means. An analogy might be if I asked a person on the street, "How many purple cows are there on Saturn?" To my knowledge there are not any purple cows, at least not born that way and the average person has never been to Saturn; therefore, how would they know the answer to the question? I would argue that the majority of people would answer that the question is absurd to begin with.

Nevertheless, the woman not only gave a reply (a serious one), she gave a reply that intuitively (for all who were present), felt like it *might* be a reasonable answer; that is unless you are an anthropologist who studies such behaviors frequently. Her reply was that "the spirits are just smarter than us." I assume by "us" she meant all living humans and not just the group of us watching the celebration. The woman's reply took almost no time and for the majority of people that were present was a sufficient answer to the question. It seems as if she possessed intuitive knowledge of her religious ritual system.

Whitehouse's statement concerning rituals highlights the empirical problem evident in the woman's reply. She didn't learn this answer in any text I have ever seen, nor heard of in this particular situation. I have heard this type of reply in various ethnographic scenarios, but not in this particular cultural

---

[1] According to Robert Smith, the first reference to the *O-bon* festival is recorded "in the *Nihon-shoki* . . . which reports that in 606 the Empress Suiko (554–628) ordered its observance in all the temples of the country" (1974, p. 15). Folk tradition states that the ritual observed in Kyoto on the last day of the *O-bon* originated when great plagues broke out in the city. The burning of the *kanji* may have initiated with the mass burning of bodies (in special ways) outside the city.

scenario. I surmise that the woman came to this conclusion naturally, without any special/extraordinary cultural education. Though the answer defies logic, it was the woman's natural *interpretation* of the situation with limited amount of information given. McCauley and Lawson (2002) identify this inferential ability in certain cultural behaviors as the "religious ritual competence" (RRC). Here they write:

> Just as speakers have robust intuitions about numerous features of linguistic strings, participants in religious ritual systems possess similar intuitive insight into the character of ritual acts. Both sorts of intuitions reflect mastery of a body of knowledge about extremely complex cultural systems. Although this knowledge for some individuals may prove to be explicitly tacit, they demonstrate their knowledge, nonetheless, through their intuitions about the form of rituals and their successful participation in them. Participants in rituals who are unable to formulate explicitly even a single rule that governs their ritual system still have many, if not most, of the requisite intuitions about ritual form. (Similarly, many native speakers cannot state even state a single rule of their grammars). (Lawson and McCauley 1990, p. 77)

In addition, humans are able to infer a range of possible religious representations and conclusions about them quite naturally with very little amount of mental expenditure, implicitly suggesting that humans are not "Blank Slates" (see Pinker 2002). It makes sense that a being that is able to make these rich inferences would prosper in the kind of environment that humans live in. Frequently, individuals are given only a handful of information and then need to make a quick yet efficient response. If we were told, "Do not cross the road unless you look left then right," we might find ourselves the recipient of The Darwin Awards,[2] if a car was coming down the wrong side of the road when we crossed or if we lived in another culture where they drive on the other side of the road. In other words, humans are incredibly proficient at adapting to situations with very little information given to them. *Interpretation* is something we do all the time, though we rarely notice that we do it.

Interpretation is so natural that it is quite easy for individuals (especially scholars) to peel away extremely salient representations from various material

---

[2] The Darwin Awards are awarded posthumously to individuals who take themselves out of the human gene pool by killing themselves in ways that exceptionally disregard common sense. See http://www.darwinawards.com/.

portraits (e.g., texts, art, observations, and architecture) claiming that these "captured" representations are capable of explaining certain cultural behaviors and/or beliefs. Many of these arguments are extremely powerful and have resulted in an enormous, yet distinct body of cultural knowledge.

Symbolic Theories

Several years ago a professor of mine, who was an expert in Indian religions, told our class an interesting story. She reported that early in her life, on a visit to India, a group (of her and her colleagues) was hiking on a trail and as they came to a crossroads, the young students noticed a large boulder dividing their path. They all talked amongst themselves and agreed there was something *special* about this rock. Several of them took out several trinkets and other smaller stones and placed them on top of the large boulder. My professor thought nothing of it, until many years had passed by, and walking down the path again one day, she came across the boulder. It was now covered with *special* objects (e.g., garlands, burnt lamps, trinkets, and stones). She remarked how odd it was that this boulder (though remarkable) now had become a shrine. She wondered if the rock was just *special*, or if people that had passed by year after year since my professor's group had placed articles upon it, had mistaken the boulder for a sacred rock.

The debate over the meaning in ritual behavior is an intensely contested topic in the human sciences, particularly anthropology. Some scholars argue that rituals are a meaningful form of behavior. Trading in symbolism, some scholars argue that, a ritual means "this (a) because of this (b)." Typically, when (a) and (b) are introduced as "types," they are examined in relationship to each other, such as male/female, hot/cold, culture/nature. These types and their relationships provide a point of reference for further intellectual inquiry, interpretation, and explanation. By doing so, scholars are able to extract systems of meaning from complex mental or cultural representations. This method is sometimes known as structuralism, and is heavily skewed in favor of binary oppositions.[3]

---

[3] The most salient forms of these arguments are explained as binary oppositions extracted from modes of behavioral clusters, comparable to sociological "ideal types" (see specifically Weber

Scholars interested in semiotics (the study of signs and symbols), for example, argue this point. The underlying principle of semiotics is that there are certain codes latent in texts, to be uncovered by hidden rules of decoding (see Sperber 1975). Moreover, it is assumed that certain material objects (signs) are inherently connected to each other, such as, to give an example, a tree might be connected to the cross that Jesus was crucified on. Others (e.g., Bloch 1974; Staal 1979, 1989, pp. 131-40) recently have argued that either ritual is so cryptic as to make the action of performing it needless (gibberish), or that the performance of a ritual is simply in toto meaningless. Here Staal writes:

> We conclude that the unchanging syntactic structures of ritual are consistent with a great variety of meanings, artificially attached to them....This abundance of meanings is tantamount to the non existence of a single intrinsic, basic and necessary meaning. Rituals, then, are different from expressions of language....Meanings are attached in haphazard ways. (Staal 1989, p. 140)

The problem of meaning in ritualized behavior is complex. As already discussed, humans are by their very nature good at inferring conclusions based upon a limited amount of information. The problem of meaning is that an individual has to extrapolate, something that goes beyond normal everyday conversation and action. This is not hard to do; however, interpretation itself eventually leads to the problem of subjectivity, which has no real explanatory power. How are scientists able to discern between subjective interpretations, which construe meaning? In addition, since interpretation appears to be easily constructed and proffered by humans, what interpretations should scientists categorize as valid and which ones (interpretations) should they leave out as invalid? Are there certain interpretations that are better interpretations than

---

1993/1922). Going back to the methodology of Malinowski's ethnographic functionalism (1922), anthropologists have used behavioral clusters—cultural phenotypes—as binary modes to theorize about cultural data (Kuper 1983, p. 194). Examples of these are numerous in the field of anthropology including: sacred/profane (É. Durkheim 1976), separation/incorporation (Hertz 1960), purity/pollution (Douglas 2005), structure/anti-structure (Turner 1995), written/oral (Goody 1987), raw/cooked (Levi-Strauss 1983) , death/rebirth (Bloch & Parry 1982) and imagistic/doctrinal (Whitehouse 2004) to name but a few. Of these seminal works, only Whitehouse has explored historical (Whitehouse & Martin 2004), ethnographic (Whitehouse & Laidlaw 2004), and most importantly experimental (Whitehouse & McCauley 2005) claims of universal features of his binary "modes" theory. All the previous social/structural modes theories relied heavily upon methods of symbolism to substantiate such claims.

others? Many scholars who employ sociological theories (e.g., Durkheim, Van Gennep, Turner, Douglas, Bloch, and Parry) argue that there are certain symbols that inherently connect and create meaning within cultural contexts. However, are certain objects able to construct such meanings?

Ritual celebrations take place almost every day all over the world; they elicit interpretations via symbols. Why are people so compelled to these behaviors? Here, Stephen Teiser elicits the point describing the ritual cousin of the Japanese *O-bon* festival, by summing up his own observations of the *Hungry Ghost* festival in Taiwan. Here he writes:

> As a complex symbolic event, the festival drew together every social class and expressed a challenging blend of values. The myths of the ghost festival were not defined in any single authoritative text or canon, nor were its ritual forms limited to a particular context. In light of this diversity, largely suppressed in previous studies, my analysis uses the festival as focus of widely held values. It is only with such a focus that the multiple meanings that the festival assumed for a broad range of people in medieval China began to appear (Teiser 1988, p. xii).

Teiser (1988) reveals that ritual behavior is so open, so free from textual, cultural, or ideological constraints that people are in all probability able to make individual meanings out of these actions at will, thus, making them publicly attractive, repeatable, and transmittable. If we are to take one of the many sociological/symbolic theories of say Victor Turner, simplified, as "rituals reinforce structure" (1995, p. 201), the analysis of Teiser makes it reasonably clear that if there is such a structure it cannot be held that there is any stability in that structure for any tangible amount of time outside of theoretical portraits (e.g., historical texts, ethnography, aesthetics, and other material evidence). This "structure" seems too fragile to elicit "laws" or "rules" consistent with say physics or mathematics. 1 must *always* equal 1 and x must *always* equal x in mathematics, or the system falls apart. This is clearly *not* the case in cultural behaviors.

Here lies the problem in a North American informant's unusual portrayal of the Catholic "Ash Wednesday" ritual:

> This year we were told that due to the amount of people wanting to participate in the Ash Wednesday rites, the Priest would be outside the Church on the sidewalk performing them to those of us who only had time to drive up

and receive them. Many members of the Church were up in arms about this, because these rites are only to be performed within the sanctum of the Church itself. Many of them referred to canon law that prohibits such behavior to the Catholic faithful. Several high ranking members refused to accept the rites, vowing to attend other Catholic Churches in town for Ash Wednesday.

Some of us joked about it saying, "Hey, the Church has to compete with McDonalds and Blackberries now." Catholics want it "our way" and they want to be able to drive up and do their religious deeds just like they want a "super combo with a biggie coke." Ash Wednesday went off without a hitch though. Even those that complained were right there. The Priest just mediated and made sure they received their rites inside the Church, but to the rest of "us heathens," the "drive through Ash" was just fine. I took the kids and we all drove up and received the rites and the priest put ash on our foreheads. The kids actually got a kick out of it, if they would just be as interested when we took them to regular Mass.

The informant's version of this rite is very insightful. The "rules" of prohibiting the rites outside of the sacred space of the Church were readily put aside, and the majority of the people simply found it more convenient to do it this way. Moreover, to the participants the ritual was successful just as if they had done it the old way, even though as some of the community pointed out it may have gone against "canon" rules.[4]

I presented a "thought experiment" (see Jablonka & Lamb 2005), similar to the "Ash Wednesday" problem, to a group of students in two large North American university classes. I asked them (about 75 students) to tell me what constituted a *successful* wedding ritual? I asked them to give me a list of things and I would write them on the board. I emphasized that these actions "had" to be in the wedding to be successful.

The students gave me between 35-40 items (per class) that had to be in a successful wedding ceremony including such agents, actions, and objects as a ring, wedding dress, presiding religious figures, witnesses, sacred vows, sacred

---

[4] I have (as of yet) been unable to find in a text (or from any priest) that such a rule exists in the Catholic Church. Though most of my informant's responses were that the local bishop could decide such things based upon the local circumstance. It is fairly reasonable that such a rule doesn't exist, since these rites are performed regularly in wartime on the battlefield and in hospitals to the sick. In addition, what seems naturally salient is that *some* participants believed there was a rule and *some* didn't care.

books, a man and a woman, special places etc. Then I asked the students to tell me if they had ever been to a successful wedding where any of these things were not present. One by one all of the beliefs written on the blackboard disappeared. Several of the students argued over certain things that were taken off, mainly due to their "beliefs" about a certain type of wedding (e.g., same-sex marriage, non-religious marriage, repeated weddings/renewed vows).

The fascinating point, however, of this empirical exercise is that out of all the beliefs that the students had about weddings, *none of them could have predicted the success of a wedding in any particular context*, extending Frits Staal's ritual claims that, "[m]eanings are attached in haphazard ways" (1989, p. 140). The individual students just "knew" when a wedding was performed correctly and when it wasn't. This problem presents an interesting dichotomy between Turner's reinforcement via ritual behavior. The students simply didn't agree on what the rules of success or failure were.

Turner (1995) argues, further, that the problem is defined best by the "dialectical process" (p. 203) between two modalities: structure and *communitas* (pp. 96–97). By extending Durkheim's theory of the social (Durkheim 1976; Durkheim & Lukes 1982), the web (cultural patterns) of the social organism utilizes ritual to constrain the individual, so that the individual is unaware that he/she increases the stability of the social organism. Furthermore, these modalities reinforce (or graft) the social fabric onto the individual (via enculturation). Turner's interest in the liminal period (the stage between separation and incorporation) of Van Gennep's "rites of passage" (1960) highlights certain structural/symbolic tendencies where structure is flipped, or reversed, in the liminal phase (Turner 1995, pp. 96–97, 183–94).

Taking my example in Chapter Four, the cremation of the body in the charnel grounds of ancient India, the cremation phase of the mortuary ritual is "in-between" separation and incorporation in Van Gennep's theory. Thus, using Turner's argument, the cemetery monks, and by extension in my analysis the *bhikkhunīs* (Pāli: nuns), social roles were reversed with the roles of the elite monks. This means then that the nuns, for the brief period of the liminal phase of cremation, were elevated to a high structural level (they were in charge); while, the elite *bhikkhus* (Pāli: monks) were demoted to inferior roles (they were not in charge of the cremation). However, once put back into the incorporation phase (i.e., when the *vihāra* monks circumambulated the *stūpa*), the social roles were once again flipped back and solidified—at least in the historical and ethnographic portrait I have painted.[5]

If Turner's analysis is correct (and I think there is *some* merit to it for reasons I will discuss shortly), the phase of *communitas* (anti-structure phase creating the social reversal) would have appeared to monastic outsiders such as the laity as extremely powerful religious roles. Therefore, the cemetery monks and *bhikkhunīs* may have been controlled by the mortuary rituals and kept within their inferior social roles; however, I argue the laity (the monastic outsiders) would not have been able to tangibly observe such structure and *communitas*, because the representations only applied to those *within* the group, not *outside* it. Moreover, such analyses do not seem sufficient for explanatory theories, since their success depends upon structure/rules contained within ethnographic/historical observations presented in texts.

What is apparent is a kind of circular reasoning. The texts are not sufficient to explain the beliefs of individuals and groups because they are not able to explain behaviors outside of the text; therefore, scholars must observe the behaviors of these individuals and groups, which then *create* "ethnographic texts" illustrating certain structures, rules, and symbols thus creating texts which are not sufficient to explain the behaviors of individuals and groups outside of these texts. An anthropological theory that relies on symbolism as a method, simply allows for circular reasoning and subjective interpretations, not explanatory theory.[6]

There is a possible alternative, one that employs natural selection as a model to explain why humans might develop the capacity to be social animals and, further, "evelop" (evolve plus develop) (see Jablonka & Lamb 2005, p. 148) social features enhancing conspecific fitness. Needless to say for social animals (humans), the question is how symbols are created, so that meaning is construed to these individuals that get shared as public representations. How do we share in our representations, thus creating culture?

---

[5] Carter suggests this problem in his forward to *Death in Banaras*, "Parry is content to let his ethnography speak for itself. He abstains from any extraneous theoretical claims, though it must be admitted that *in these postmodern times this in itself amounts to a theoretical claim about the capacity of ethnographic writing to represent reality* (Parry 1994, p. xv) (my italics).

[6] As Pals offers in his analysis of Clifford Geertz, there is the tendency to "over-interpret meanings rather than explain facts" in regard to ethnographic data (Pals 2006, p. 287).

Symbolism: When Representations Collide

In *Rethinking Symbolism* (1975), Dan Sperber argues that semiological theories are not adequate explanations of symbolic behavior. In fact, Sperber claims that symbolism is a specific and distinct cognitive process that connects representations in the mind-brain that are represented neither encyclopedically nor in our cognitive "dictionaries." So, symbolism is the process that associates representations when neither definitions nor descriptions find their application (Sperber 1996, pp. 71–72, 146–50; 2000). Therefore, symbolism is a process that takes place in the mind; meaning is constructed by individuals and groups in culture. Symbolism is not meaning. Arguments that rely on theories of symbolism and derive meanings from these theories are unreliable, *since humans are able to make meaning out of almost anything.* One way of putting this is that symbolism can take place even without meaning.

To illustrate the point, many advocates of symbolism argue that certain objects/signs are inherently related to other material objects either through "motivations" or motivational interpretations (Sperber 1975, pp. 23–34). Sperber calls this kind of theory the "cryptological" argument. Cryptological arguments are fallacious because they presume that certain public representations are related to other public representations (via origins and motivations). Example, it is reasonable for any person who has taken algebra, to know that x can stand for any known variable. Therefore if $x=3$ and $2x+1 = y$, then a person might deduce that $y = 7$. However, it would be erroneous to think that x is inherently related to the number 3 outside of a public and very material connection by the properties of higher math. These variables and numbers only make sense inside the construct that algebra allows.

This connection can take place one of two ways. Either it happens in the material world, where someone such as a teacher writes on a blackboard that *this* stands for *that*, as in mathematics. Or, as in the case of many ritual behaviors, this *connection* takes place within the human mind (connecting private representations). Outside of the mind making these connections (public or private), nothing is really connected (Sperber 1996, p. 43). Let us look at another cultural example.

Some scholars of religion over the years have argued that the Cross is a universal symbol. The famous historian of religions, Mircea Eliade (1996) claimed that these types of symbols (e.g., *axis mundi*) were the basic building block of religiosity (also Myth and Ritual). Therefore, before and after the Christian Jesus, the cross symbolically stood for various things (e.g., tree, center of the world, ladder to heaven etc.). Sperber adds, why can't the cross stand for the "symbol of a crime, because so many criminals also died on it" (1975, p. 28)? Specifically, which cross are we talking about? There is quite a difference between *per se* a tree and the poles made to crucify the Christian Jesus. Yes, it was probably made of wood; yes, it might be said to have the characteristics of a tree, but might there also be more differences than similarities? In addition, might there be multiple connections concerning representations?

What about the distinction between trees as living things and a tree that is used to kill people (as in a Cross)? Furthermore, which cross are we talking about; a cross of crucifixions, the Red Cross, the Iron Cross, St. John's Cross etc.? St. Andrew's cross (on the Scottish flag) appears just as much as an "X" turned on its side rather than a cross. How about a + sign in mathematics? All of these have cultural and historical contexts where someone, somewhere connected these things. Not only are they not inherently connected, what about representations that were never connected?

Very few people go around saying that a soda bottle is a symbol for Jesus on the Cross. Although, it should be stated that people regularly find such things (such as the Virgin Mary) in grilled cheese sandwiches, wood patterns, and clouds. Nevertheless, this kind of connection says more about our cognitive predisposition to perceive agents readily, than it does for signs (see Dawkins 2006, p. 89; see Guthrie 1995). These objects themselves are not related outside of people's minds or by material culture that represents a public representation of the human mind. A plus sign (+) clearly doesn't denote anything but addition within mathematics. It would be absurd to say that the mathematic problem $2x + 2y = 10$ is a *secret* code for the cross on which Jesus hung because there is a plus sign in it.

Many scholars have of course tried such things, resulting in the publication of bestselling books, computer programs, and research agendas trying to prove that these *semiological* connections exist. However, even if such code cracking endeavors were found to be correct, someone or something had to put it into the code and hope that later on someone or something would *crack* it. That of course is the hope of many who ultimately think it is the work of intelligent design. However, as Richard Dawkins (1996) argues, these things too can be explained sufficiently by the theory of natural selection.

All of these theories still imply the very important work of Sperber that there are no symbols, which are inherently created. The representations must be connected within the mind, or by extension of the mind, public representations. Therefore, ritual behavior is not inherently meaningful; it is meaningful or meaningless because individual participants construe it that way (1996, pp. 41–43). Furthermore, as Staal argues, "[r]itual is pure activity, without meaning or goal" in and of itself (1989, p. 131). This may in fact be why successful ritualized behaviors are able to elicit such multiple meanings and powerful lasting public and private representations. They do not in fact have their own meaning; they need people to give it to them.

Functional Theories

Why are mortuary rituals social behaviors?

Émile Durkheim (1858–1918) argues that the role of a dead body represents danger to society and social institutions. His work on *Suicide* (1951) and *The Elementary Forms of Religious Life* (1976) suggests that in the presence of individual death, the community feels compelled through a "collective unconscious" to deal with the dead body in a way that brings the individual's social roles, resources, and identity back into the realm of the social (Bloch & Parry 1982, pp. 3–4). Durkheim's argument is premised on the individual as defined by the social fabric constrained/grafted upon him/her. The individual is defined (for Durkheim) as the sum total of this social identity. Individuals, moreover, operate on a "special social psychology" that is distinct from individual personality and psychology that reinforces a "collective unconscious" observable in *special* "social facts" (Durkheim & Lukes 1982, pp. 39–40). Social facts are defined as what people actually do, say, and feel empirically in the world that can be observed (Kinney & Gilday 2000, p. 166).

After the death of an individual, according to Durkheim, the group (i.e., social organism) constrains the danger of the individual's death by performing a religious ceremony that involves particular kinds of rituals emphasizing the social order. Durkheim argues that there are perfectly good social explanations for ceremonies surrounding death, explaining that the individuality of death presents the collective organism with an explicit danger (biology) that threatens the organism's cohesion and stability. Rituals, (or piacular/mourning rites) following a death reaffirm this individual loss as a problem for society but, by ritually redistributing the individual's public identity back into the collective order, mitigates the threat of social disintegration. Religious concepts and the rituals they inform were, and are, created for the purpose of reinforcing a social group's cohesion. As Jack Goody asserts, individual acts are best seen "as a part of a total system of social relationships, a standpoint that even the best informed and most sensitive participant finds difficult to take" (1962, p. 38).[7] Goody further claims that, "of great importance here are the social control functions of ceremonials. Funerals are inevitably occasions for summing up an individual's social personality" (p. 29).

Emotional Theories

Malinowski adds that society has to overcome the instincts of individuals, who in bouts of emotional stress would destroy the social fabric; therefore, humans need the beliefs and behaviors of magic and religion to save the community from certain collapse (Malinowski 1948, p. 87). Here he claims:

> If the view here taken of the biological function of religion is true, some such similar role must also be played by the whole mortuary ritual....The strong tendency...to give way to fear and horror, to abandon the corpse, to run away from the village, to destroy all the belongings of the dead one—all these impulses exist, and if given way would be extremely dangerous, disintegrating the group, destroying the material foundations of culture. Death in a primitive society is, therefore, much more than the removal of a member. By setting in motion one part of the deep forces of the instinct of self-preservation, it threatens the vary cohesion and the solidarity of the group....In short, religion here assures the victory of tradition and culture over the mere negative response of thwarted instinct. (Malinowski 1948, pp. 52-53)

---

[7] It is important to note that Goody (1962) is incredibly critical of Durkheim's social theory of religion, although, he implores a "modes" theory similar to Durkheim's student, Robert Hertz's work (1960) and Durkheim's contemporary Arnold Van Gennep (1960) (see specifically p. 46).

Malinowski, of course, argues that Durkheim's sociology was perhaps the product of the culture of his time. Where Durkheim and his follower's construed their theory upon modern Western ideals of democracy and the newly popular sociology "on everyone's lips" (Pyysiäinen 2003, p. 56), thus explaining every phenomena by "collective forces," similar to a child with a new hammer, pounding away at everything in sight (Malinowski 1948, p. 56).

Functional/Emotional theories, like Malinowski's, are problematic since they predicate the behavior of ritualized actions like mortuary rituals on emotions like fear, disgust, anger, sadness etc. Here Parker Pearson furthers the emotional argument:

> The fear of the dead is a regular feature of liminal time prior to the rites of incorporation. Whether we weep for the dead because we fear them or we fear the dead because we weep for them, the dead are *universally* a source of fear, *especially during the corpse's putrefaction*. With the passing of time, the deceased may come to be venerated, and fear and veneration may go hand and hand. Places of the dead such as tombs and graveyards may also provide a material locus for *feelings* of dread and fear. The separation of the corpse from the living is one means by which fear of the dead is *controlled*. Many ethnographic studies allude to strategies designed to sever connections with the deceased. (Parker Pearson 1999, pp. 25) (my emphasis)

What we know from multiple ethnographic sources is that emotions such as fear and sadness are not universal reactions by individuals in mortuary behavior (Metcalf & Huntington 1991, pp. 43–61). In addition, though, Durkheim has argued that mourning and related emotional behavior are based upon social/functional relations. Social/Functional theorists claim that crying/wailing is a public display of the social grafting itself upon the individual; it is not random emotional behavior but these types of responses occur at special times that indicate their importance to strengthen the social. Here Durkheim says:

> [M]ourning is not the spontaneous expression of individual emotions. If the relations weep, lament, mutilate themselves, it is not because they feel themselves personally affected by the death of their kinsman....Mourning is not a natural movement of private feelings wounded by a cruel loss; it is the duty imposed by the group. One weeps, not simply because he is forced to weep. It is a ritual attitude, which he is forced to adopt out of respect for custom...this

obligation is sanctioned by mythical or social penalties (Durkheim 1976, pp. 442–43).

Nonetheless, these emotional responses are not found everywhere in the world in the same way. Some cultures actually respond to dead bodies with laughter, which can be seen in wakes of New Orleans, Ireland and Nyakyusa mortuary customs (G. Wilson 1939), or the violent behavior of participants by beating, cutting, burning, or wounding themselves or others (Durkheim 1976, p. 446), or the sadistic shaking, spiting, or handling the corpse in a rough and furious manner (Bloch 1982; Stephen 1988). As Metcalf and Huntington, both anthropologists claim, the "[u]niformity of human emotion does not explain the rituals of societies" (1991, p. 61). Emotions themselves are too broad of a term (see Ledoux, 1998, p. 21), too widely used and distributed to explain ritualized actions that are highly rigid, non-haphazard, and goal oriented.

Both Malinowski and Durkheim, however, who have made important anthropological theories, utilize biological metaphors in their data. On the one hand, Malinowski uses the powerful role of biological emotions and the functional theory that religion controls these emotional individual hazards for the sake of culture. On the other hand, Durkheim also makes use of analogies to a biological theory in order to make claims at the level of the social fact. In both *The Elementary Forms of Religious Life* (1976) and *Suicide* (1951), his social theory mimics the form of biological metaphor because he conceives of society as analogous to an organism with individuals representing elements of the organism. We might assume that humans, in Durkheim's claims are similar to Harvester Ants and Bees; although, humans have culture, where the insects only have instinct.[8] While social theory is Durkheim's aim, more than one scholar has noted there is more than a trace of this biological analogy in his collective approach (see Morris 1987, p. 120).

---

[8] I disagree with Sperber's use of social and cultural as interchangeable (1996, pp. 11–16). I believe this promotes less clarity, when it should claim more. I argue that "social" is equivalent to the various functional interactions between individuals which produce "culture"—material products (or by-products) seen in texts (here a text may refer to an action, belief, or artifact). Though I have taken a "materialist" stance, I don't deny Sperber's salient point that private representations are in fact just as much material (and cultural for that matter) as public representations .

To say that Durkheim sees society as an organism means only that he uses biology as a metaphor or model, not that he's theorizing at the biological level of analysis. Though, as discussed previously, Malinowski concerned himself with this level of abstraction. The kinds of explanations offered by scholars since Durkheim (e.g., Hertz, Van Gennep, Douglas, Turner, Goody, Bloch, and Geertz) have remained firmly at the level of this social fact and are most often concerned with how rituals *function* and what they symbolize or mean. In fact Bloch and Parry, who operate on a Durkheimian model, claim that the two analyses (sociological and symbolic) "need to be combined" (1982, pp. 6–7). However, taking evolution into account for Durkheim's sociology (and it begs the question on whether Durkheim might have been aware of Darwin's theory of evolution? [Darwin 1859]), we might ask *why* or *how* are humans *biologically* social creatures under the rubric of Durkheim's larger sociological theory?

Few scholars would debate that humans are social creatures. Everyday individuals can walk out their doors and they are functionally attached in almost every way to other individuals. Nevertheless, how is it that humans became this way? Natural selection provides a starting point. It makes good sense to argue that over the last several hundred thousand years humans interacted with each other in complex ways, they survived longer by sharing and exploiting resources and were more successful spreading their genes (and memes), thus, enhancing fitness. To accommodate this new social lifestyle over time, humans needed a sophisticated "social intelligence" to evolve at the same time as they became more socially complex (Mithen 1996).

Natural selection claims that in order for a species to evolve as a complex being, it usually develops from simple to composite (Dawkins 2006, p. 150–51). *If* there is such a thing as a "social organism" (and I am cautiously skeptical), *then* can it not be studied at a lower level of abstraction, namely its aggregates? "Science explains things in terms of the interactions of simpler things, ultimately the interactions of fundamental particles" (Dawkins 2006, p. 147).

As in the analogy of liver cells, which operate within the liver (*in vivo*) differently than outside the liver (*in vitro*), *in vivo* cells operate in a type of collective with other *in vivo* liver cells making the organ of the liver function properly. However, once taken out of the liver and put into a petrie dish (*in vitro*), they are able to survive even replicate (with degeneration), though they do not function in the same way as *in vivo* liver cells. These cells have problems responding to environmental stimuli and they act differently.[9] *In vitro* cells, on the other hand, can be put into other organs such as the kidney and they do not survive for very long, nor work with *in vivo* kidney cells (Koniaris et al. 2003, pp. 637–38).

This suggests that kidney cells and liver cells have evolved by natural selection to operate specifically for a certain organ and its function. These cells are the product of ontogeny recapitulating phylogeny, in that they are cells that were/are selected to operate in the liver and only the liver. These cells are unable to work, except in their respective organs because they simply evolved that way. The liver itself doesn't cause the liver cells to do anything. They were selected to be liver cells and help the liver function properly.

It is fair to note that physicians are experts on humans and their organs, and general systems; however, it is biologists who study lower level models of abstraction (cells). Both are experts on the human body; however, it is the lower level research (biology) that generates a "mature" corpus of knowledge based upon the science of the human body (Kuhn 1996, pp. 10–11).

Physicians, of course, are extremely well trained and knowledgeable about human anatomy from a variety of higher level abstractions. Nevertheless, if anthropologists and other cultural experts study the "social organism," then can't other behavioral experts (e.g., biologists, psychologists, and cognitive scientists) study lower level modes of the social organism's aggregates?[10] I, along with others (e.g., Mort & Slone 2006), submit they can and should. The natural sciences allow for this kind of important research.

The Evolution of the Social Mind

Pre-modern humans probably had specific systems that handled day to day problems as seen in the behaviors of primates (e.g., hunting and foraging patterns, simple tool making, and mate selection techniques). Steven Mithen (1996) has argued forcefully that modern humans developed a "generalized

---

[9] As one biologist quipped, "they don't know which way is up" (personal communication, Mckillop, 2007).

[10] See Popper (1972) for specific arguments on explanatory theories involving methodological individualism.

cognitive system" that evolved from a more ancestral and specialized cognitive system (the "Swiss army knife" model), where modern humans developed the benefit of fluidity between specific systems that earlier humans and primates didn't have. This cognitive fluidity (especially social intelligence) explains the human propensity for complex social behavior, but also products (or by-products) such as language, art, religion, writing, and symbolism.[11]

So, taking Mithen's claims into account, Durkheim's theory concerning the social organism is best explained by the process of natural selection, where humans over time (phylogeny) became social creatures, but more importantly evolved a sophisticated, but cognitively fluid, mental architecture that empha-sized social intelligence for conspecific fitness. Therefore, not only were other individuals (agents) important to human mental systems, dead bodies, which were individuals, now objects, stimulate these same systems to produce rich inferences between cognitively fluid specialized mental tools that are able to handle them. Even so, when do these essential systems develop and are they adaptable for human fitness? It would seem, then, that mortuary behaviors might have practical value for enhancing conspecific fitness in humans.

Practical Theories

Though it is sometimes overlooked, some scholars have tried to claim theories that explain behavior towards dead bodies as practical. Put simply, they claim that humans wish to get rid of corpses for clinical reasons. Bodies like other animal meat, once decaying and rotten, smell bad. People also don't want to look at a dead body lying around; so, they perform certain behaviors to dis-pose of it. Nevertheless, they don't want to treat a dead body as just another piece of garbage; therefore, they treat the body in a way that separates its re-moval from ordinary disposal (e.g., trash, spoiled food, and other waste prod-ucts).

Actually, the argument for practical theories of disposal of dead bodies is directly related to *intellectualist* arguments for religion. Tylor and Frazier

---

[11] Dunbar adds, "My own view is that [language] evolved to facilitate bonding through the ex-change of social information, and was later hijacked for use in these semi-religious contexts in such a way as to formalize what may have well been pre-existing practices [ritualized behavior]" (1996, p. 147) (my brackets). See also Donald (1991).

claimed that early religious beliefs were simply "primitive" explanations for unknown things (Frazier 1911; Tylor 1871). In other words, causes for unexplained phenomena were rationalized by early humans and so *religious* ideas and behaviors were a way in which to orient the world around them. By extension, corpses just smell horrible and no one wants to look at their sister lying around the house drawing the flies, or worse—predators. So, in order to treat them as something more than trash, we pay homage to them by performing a ritual for them; thus eliminating the bad odor, the person, the guilt, and the problem. We also make ourselves feel better about not throwing a friend or relative out like the garbage.

However, as Pascal Boyer has claimed, *intellectualist* arguments for religious belief and practice produce more questions than they answer (Boyer 2001, pp. 10-19). Questions like, what happens to the person once they are disposed of through ritual behavior? Where do they go? Who else is there? How long has there (i.e., heaven) been around? etc. It makes sense that there are practical reasons for disposing of dead bodies; however, many societies go to such great lengths to perform these actions, utilizing valuable time and resources that the practical explanations for mortuary behavior simply do not seem to justify these actions cross-culturally. Ergo, Boyer proffers a naturalist explanation for this cross-cultural behavior where dead bodies activate various cognitive systems, producing a by-product result of normal mental activity (2001, pp. 203-28).

It is also important to note that not *all* individuals and societies are disgusted by dead bodies. Some individuals and groups engage in actions that kiss and touch the corpse, throw themselves onto the dead body, smear liquids from the corpse onto themselves, and keep the departed near or even inside their homes. Practical theories for the ritualized disposal of dead bodies do not appear sufficient for an explanatory theory of mortuary ritual behavior.

Problems

Why these theories don't work

In short, the dominant theories of the last hundred years or so (e.g., social, symbolic, functional, emotional, and practical), while suggestive, do not appear to be able to *explain* why cross cultural mortuary behaviors occur. Frequently, these theories rely on arguments from symbolist theorizing, which as I previously claimed come so naturally to humans that they are able to make meaning out of almost anything. If ritualized behavior is by definition a highly rigid, non-haphazard, and goal-demoted activity, then theories that rely on a random series of events and emotional predispositions are neither necessary nor sufficient for explanatory scientific type theories. Ritualized behavior (as Staal has suggested and I have claimed) may in fact be transmittable precisely because they don't have meaning inherently attached to them and, therefore, are open to numerous individual interpretations. Therefore, latent social-functional theories that use ritual to do anything (via motivations) are nearly impossible, since there is nothing in ritual behavior to do (much less caused to do) outside of "pure activity." In other words, ritual(s) does not and cannot "do" anything in and of itself; humans use ritual(s) (as a tool) to "do" things to themselves. Many times this involves individual and collective representations, which humans place on the ritual as if it acts as an agent. Nevertheless, ritual is not an agent.[12]

Summary

In Chapter Six, I argued that religious ritualized behavior cannot be universally explained by the cultural tokens produced by the participants themselves. Humans utilized a natural process of interpretation in addition to learned cultural information to explain ritual events. In fact, much of the process of interpretation is not the product of learned cultural information but an aggregate of complex mental tools that evolved to "handle" specific tasks. I ar-

---

[12] Humphrey and Laidlaw have taken the opposing view of ritual. Here they argue, "Ritual actors, we have said, are not directly authors of their acts, and their individual intentions do not define what it is they do. Ritual is obviously social and cultural, not just the sum of the beliefs and desires of individuals and their consequent actions." (1994, p. 261). Although this Durkhemian stance (i.e., outside-in cognition) by Humphrey and Laidlaw is widely held in social and cultural anthropology, I am hesitant to award "culture" counterintuitive agency. Is culture really a superhuman agent, which acts upon individuals and groups? It should be noted that although I disagree with many of their conclusions, I find Humphrey and Laidlaw's data on Jain *pūjā* exciting and significant for explanatory theories on ritualized and ritual behavior. Perhaps, a cognitive ethnography of the same data would have resulted in drastically different results.

gued further that humans have the natural ability to generate answers with only limited information available to them. Therefore, interpretation and meaning are naturally occurring processes that coincide with learned cultural information.

Finding meaning in a culture is not a difficult thing to do. In fact, humans are so naturally proficient at generating meaning we might wish to conclude that humans are "meaning-making creatures." Ritualized actions are an exciting display of human behavior. For over a hundred years, anthropologists have proposed creative theories on the reasons behind such ornate displays of behavior (from intellectualist, social, symbolic, functional, emotional, and practical perspectives); however, none of them have been able to circumvent ethnographic data negating their hypotheses. This weakness is not due to a lack of clarity of their arguments. It seems that these theories suffer from problems in the methodology of ethnography and the fact that like—their participants—they are themselves meaning-making creatures, susceptible to imposing rich interpretations on to available cultural data. Much of anthropological theory at present is (for better or worse) social/symbolic—relying heavily on "unpacking" meanings from a given culture.

Anthropological studies provided a very useful lens for the analysis of cultural data. In fact, because of the rich ethnographic work carried out by anthropologists for over a century all over the world, scientists, especially evolutionary and experimental psychologists, were able to discern between important features of human social intelligence and cultural "noise." Ethnography allowed scholars to ask better questions about cultural belief and behavior. Nevertheless, rarely has attention been paid to the mental processes of individuals in current anthropological research. Mental processes were (and are) in fact very much a large component of culture, "mental culture."

In Chapter Six, I employ diverse anthropological theories and methods to argue that ritualized human behavior is a product of various mental processes, many of these regarding the theory of moving things, or agents. By looking at culture through the lens of individual minds, I proffer that scientists should be interested in the evolution of social intelligence, predation, and "hazard-precaution" systems. In making this argument, I do not propose *ontological* individualism (i.e., the parts are equal to the sum). In fact, I argue for *methodo-*

logical individualism, in that ritualized behavior cannot be explained without appealing to the evolved cognitive architecture of individual human minds.

Rituals (like languages) are found in every known culture throughout the world spanning thousands (and possibly tens of thousands) of years. Rituals are often closely guarded by their cultural custodians, religious experts and institutions. Nevertheless, ritualized behaviors appear to observers as quite peculiar in that ritualized behavior is erratic, compulsive, and non-utilitarian. In this chapter, I argue that ritualized behavior is a common feature of social animals (including, but not limited to, humans).

This behavior is natural to humans but variable and in any given culture these actions might look quite different from special behaviors in another culture in different ecological circumstances. Ritualized and ritual behaviors are meaningless in and of themselves; however, due to their social nature and the strong production of meanings by participants, these actions are used by individuals and groups as a tool for socialization within groups. Moreover, rituals are used by humans to socially and culturally define the agency of biological individuals, their roles in society, different phases of biological change throughout their lifetime, and even in death to protect human culture from extinction.

Chapter Seven

Evolutionary Disgust

Question: Why would the disposal of dead bodies be adaptive?

In *Religion Explained*, Pascal Boyer claims that dead bodies are environmental triggers of several mental systems bequeathed by evolution. These systems, he argues, account for the tendency of people to display certain specifiable responses in the presence of dead bodies and to perform "special" actions on them (2001, pp. 203–8). Boyer names five systems that might be activated by the presence of a dead body. These are the Animacy, Predation, Intuitive Psychology, Person-file, and the Contagion systems (see *Figure* 7.1).

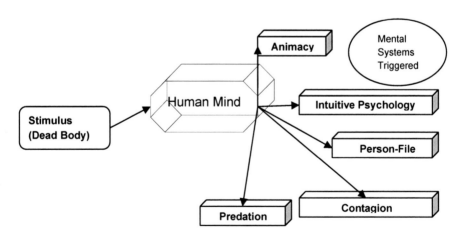

Figure 7.1 Boyer's Model of Systems Activated by Corpse Stimuli

Are Dead Bodies Dangerous?

In keeping with an evolutionary perspective, Boyer pays particular attention to the experiments that Paul Rozin (Rozin et al. 1993) and his colleagues have conducted in an attempt to establish the presence and workings of the Contagion-avoidance system. Rozin claims that humans are prone to disgust (reflex mechanism) when exposed to certain types of dangerous stimuli, causing the upper lip to lift up and cover the nostrils and the tongue to protrude outside the mouth, protecting the person from inhalation and ingestion of the noxious stimuli (Darwin 1998; Rozin 1997; Rozin & Fallon 1987).

Boyer reasons that dead bodies give off similar types of dangerous toxins (sulfur and ammonia among others) that trigger biological intuitions in the human mind, signaling the presence of danger (Boyer 2001, pp. 212–15; Rozin et al. 1993). This would seem to explain why people typically have a tendency, sometimes verging on compulsion, to handle dead bodies with great caution and dispose of them in special ways. This tendency also justifies the view that such behavior has adaptive value for human conspecific fitness. However, there are problems with this account because of certain empirical facts. I can best illustrate the problem by referring to a specific recent historical event.

Does mortuary behavior remove the threat of disease?

In December of 2004, a great tidal wave (tsunami) struck the coast of several south and southeastern Asian countries, killing over one hundred thousand people. While this disaster was of epic proportions, media reports maintained that the "proper" disposal of the dead was crucial for preventing an epidemic, insect infestation, and contamination of the water supply. Some of this information was relayed straight from disaster relief organizations "on the ground" and by various experts in disaster relief.

Local inhabitants scrambled to collect the bodies for mass burial and religious experts devised special ritual ways in which to bury them, despite calls by state authorities to delay such actions that might compromise accurate accounts of the dead. These responses to the putative danger posed by corpses are peculiar because both the World Health Organization and the Centers for

Disease Control and Prevention (presumably the world's experts on disasters involving humans) recently released scientific information stating that dead bodies resulting from natural disasters were not as dangerous as people intuitively felt they were. Here is a clear case of our intuitive responses overriding the scientific evidence. No matter what the evidence seems to imply, humans do not appear readily able to accept these notions over their own intuitive inferences. This might suggest an evolutionary type of response where it is more beneficial for humans to act according to their "gut" feelings for reasons of conspecific fitness, rather than rely on information that might be dangerous to their survival.[1]

Evidence to the contrary

Dead bodies are possible biohazards (possible infectious diseases, insect infestation etc.), but not on the scale warranted by media reports and authorities. In fact, the WHO and CDC reports indicated that dead bodies were not the main problem at all for disaster relief. The main problem was the "psychological trauma" to the living that the presence of dead bodies caused (de Ville de Goyet 2004; Fisher 2005; Harvey 2002; Morgan 2004; P.A.H.O. 2003, 2004; Wisner B. & Adams 2002). Here Morgan and Fisher write:

> Historically, epidemics resulting in mass casualties have only occurred from a few diseases, including plague, cholera, typhoid, tuberculosis, anthrax, and smallpox. As previously stated such infections are no more likely to be present in disaster victims than in the general population. Furthermore, although some of these diseases are highly contagious, their causative agents are unable to survive long in the human body following death. It is therefore unlikely that such epidemics will result from contact with a cadaver. Indeed, survivors present a much more important reservoir for disease. (Morgan 2004, p. 308)

Here the living rather than the dead are the problem.

---

[1] See specifically *Blink* (Gladwell 2005). Here Gladwell claims that people are extremely good at making quick, instinct like decisions (i.e., non-reflective intuitions) that are beneficial for their survival and livelihood the majority of the time. Like Forest Gump's character in the motion picture of the same name, "Thinking gets you killed." Also see (Damasio 1995; Ledoux 1998, pp. 36-37) for these same types of arguments.

Where there are many fatalities, the collection and disposal of bodies becomes an urgent need. This is not usually due to any health-related risks,
which are likely to be negligible, *but is important because of the possible social and
political impact and trauma. So, emergency relief teams should primarily be concerned
with the mental health of the community and its need to carry out the cultural obligations and traditions to take care of the dead, rather than potential disease transmission.* (Fisher 2005, p. 1)(emphasis added)

According to this report and others like it, dead bodies are not as dangerous to
the living as one might think. There are certain pathogens a body can carry as
long as the tissue still lives (insignificant cause for serious concern), but these
problems are not as great as one is led to believe, especially in dead bodies. In
fact, it is not because these bodies are dead that makes them dangerous. If a
dead body has an infectious disease, it was just as infectious when the person
was alive, if not more so (as a moving and interacting host), than its dead
counterpart.

This is why corpses were thought to be highly contagious in the outbreak
of the Marburg virus in Africa. The corpses were not deadly because they were
corpses, they were deadly because the bodies were infectious when the bodies
were alive and continued to be for a short period after death. In fact, of greater
worry was the potential living carrier of the virus being present at the funeral.
More importantly, many mortuary rituals across cultures involve the kissing,
touching, and/or close proximity of the living to the corpse.

In the Tsunami example, reaction by the people was to bury the dead as
quickly as possible despite governmental pleas that a proper account of the individuals take place before any such burials occured. Mass burials are generally
preferred over cremation in such cases since cremation takes an excessive
amount of resource material (wood, coal, etc.) to burn the body properly
(Fisher 2005, pp. 2–3). However, mass burials are a perceived problem for relief organizations because they believe this tends to contaminate the water
supply (by putting them upstream or in mass graves without the proper lin-
ings). However, this fact is debated and considered by many experts to be extremely negligible (p. 2).

According to the scientific evidence, though, dead bodies are not what
produce the greatest challenge for these relief organizations. What can be a
difficulty is the "psychological trauma" to the living. This isn't surprising since

dead bodies are nasty, gross, rotten, smell horrendous etc. Nevertheless, smell (and by extension toxicity) is not the reason why the people in these countries felt compelled to bury these bodies at all costs and often ritually perform these actions.

The Smell of Death

Using Rozin's facial/disgust experiments, Boyer argues that modern humans may be unconsciously aware of the potential toxicity of dead bodies. Furthermore, humans who kept away from possible pathogens in the environment lived to spread their genes another day, an obvious adaptive advantage (Boyer 2001, pp. 119-20, 214-15). Experimental studies have shown that humans do indeed have a contagion system at work (Rozin 1976; Rozin et al. 1993). These studies show that properties of the whole contagion are transferred to other objects.

For example, no matter how many times human subjects wash a glass with hot water after a cockroach has been seen in the glass, these same humans do not wish to drink from it, not too mention other glasses or foods within the vicinity of the contagious agent (cockroach). In fact, individuals will frequently wash the glass repeatedly (similar to Obsessive–Compulsive Disorder (OCD) behaviors) to alleviate their anxiety about possible pollution. Certainly there is no smell leftover in the glass; however, suggestion may have played a role in informing the subject's behavior. I suggest, when an agent is involved (cockroach), this is a much more salient representation for contagion/disgust to be activated than a representation sans an agent, such as dirt, or a human by-product such as fecal matter (which is a biologically toxic substance). A leper (agent) will almost always trigger more contagion-avoidance/disgust to an individual than a dirty glass of water. Humans may be more predisposed to respond (especially with regards to contagion/disgust) to situations that involve agents.

In fact, as Miller (1997) proffers, disgust has culturally bound properties based upon social relationships, interaction, and categorization. Thus, any anthropology of disgust must take into account the mental categorization of culture by agents and for agents. Nevertheless, as some leading theorists in this field have suggested, disgust is either purely at the cultural level (i.e., Douglas

2005) imprinted upon human minds in each localized context, or disgust is a precautionary biological warning system to save the individual and/or group from disease or extinction. It is quite clear that "disgust" is not simply a biological threat, nor is it purely manufactured by culture. It seems that disgust may be a salient starting point for the intersection between biology and culture and their influence upon each other.

Suggestion has been shown to have a major role in experimental studies, especially concerning emotional stimuli such as fear, anxiety, hunger etc. (Ledoux 1998, pp. 51–52, 61–62). Furthermore, empirical evidence like the cockroach example provides proof of unconscious suggestion (of an agent that should not be in the location that it is), but not smell. I want to qualify that smell might be useful for certain cues (i.e., mating preferences), but not in regard to dead bodies. The Boyer/Rozin theory argues that humans unconsciously are stimulated by noxious smells and tastes to cover the nose with the upper lip and protrude the tongue from the mouth, in order to prevent any possible pathogens from entering the body through the nose or mouth. One noted problem is with one of the more dangerous biohazards connected with humans, that of fecal matter.

Fecal matter is well known for its transmission of diseases (e.g., Hepatitis, HIV, bacterial agents); however, experimental research has shown that little children under the age of two years do not find fecal matter to be disgusting; they do not appear to elicit the same facial expressions as adults do (Rozin 1997; Rozin et al. 1993). This evidence suggests that disgust may be a developmental feature. Furthermore, there are some empirical problems with the contagion/disgust theory that need to be addressed.

Dead bodies produce several types of smell that humans might find unpleasant. These may depend upon the type of death and the state of the corpse. Nevertheless two odors that are produced by dead bodies are sulfur and ammonia. These two odors are peculiar because they are found in other types of environments, which do not cause ritual behaviors like mortuary rituals and certainly do not cause humans to think they are putrid or dangerously contagious.

The first is ammonia, a common chemical used in many household cleaners. Ammonia is an alkaline substance, which when used to clean, say a bathroom, that bathroom is thought to be clean, pure. Certainly it is not toxically contagious, though we might feel clean after we leave or touch an ammonia cleaned bathroom. Make no mistake that ammonia, left in the right environ-ment, is a dangerous chemical substance. Why would ammonia in one situa-tion (a corpse) be polluted, and one situation (the clean bathroom) be clean and safe?

The second odor (sulfur) can be found at many beaches near sulfur springs (Key West, Florida, for example), where hundreds of people everyday enjoy their vacations. Once again the sulfur connected with the dead body produces a putrid smell when associated with a dead body, but is an odor that is tolerable when associated with the beach. This anecdotal evidence would seem to suggest that the smell itself is not the deciding factor, whether an odor is putrid or pure. Quite the contrary, it seems that it is the association of the smell with other physical or conceptual stimuli that makes the odor patho-genic or not to humans.

In a recent empirical experiment, Bill Bass, head of the world's premier forensic lab for the decomposition of human bodies at the University of Ten-nessee at Knoxville, observed that almost none of his subjects could smell various decomposing corpses until they were in close proximity of the dead body itself (Bass 2003, p. 118). In fact, almost every subject was observed to smell the corpse only after seeing it, or realizing what the test was measuring. Though this is a crude experiment, Bass's former student, Arpad Vass, is cur-rently "working to isolate and identify the specific molecules that constitute the distinctive odor of death" (Bass 2003, p. 144; Vass et al. 2004).[2]

If dead bodies do produce odors that humans are unconsciously aware of that makes humans dispose of them in special ways, then why do humans not dispose of all animals, as well as humans, in special ways? Though humans and animals are quite different, the anatomy of say a deer is not that different from a human's. Many of the same odors would be present at the death of an ani-mal, as would at a human's demise. However, humans do not seem to dispose of most animals the same way in which they do humans. An exception is the

---

[2] Since the early drafts of this manuscript, Vass and his colleagues (2004) have defined 424 "odor signatures" associated with the decomposition of dead bodies. Their goal is to reproduce "canine olfaction" in portable forensic instruments. It is not entirely clear if (a) humans can "smell" any of these "odor signatures," or (b) if canines actually smell increased "odor signa-tures" of living people.

often times special disposal of domesticated animals like dogs, cats, fish, and birds.

My own relatives have several of the family's deceased dogs buried in the backyard complete with a stone to mark the grave. These dogs were neither embalmed, nor did a professional mortician perform the burial. My grandmother simply buried the dogs after they died. Moreover, many people have either witnessed or seen a funeral for a child's pet fish, where the family flushes the fish down the toilet in an action resembling a very basic mortuary ritual. Do fish smell like humans and animals at death? Or are these actions caused by certain types of mental systems related to the connection between the living and the dead.

Domesticated pets are very often treated like a member of the family, resulting in being treated the same way in death as they were in life. Pets tend to eat at the same time as the family, they get gifts at holidays, they receive toys to play with, and many times they recieve mortuary rituals when they die. The elaborateness of the ritual probably depends upon the amount of time and connection between the pet and their relationship with family individuals and the group. This anecdotal and empirical evidence seems to suggest that the smell of the agent/object involved has little to do with ritual behavior towards it.

The Biology of Pollution and the Behavior of Disgust

Another good example of the evidence against smell directly causing dead bodies to produce contagion/disgust for the living is the example of the *titan arum* plant, or "Corpse Flower" indigenous to Sumatra. The *titan arum* is given its name because it gives off a smell that mimics that of a dead animal in order to attract certain insects to pollinate the plant. John Kress, the chairman of the Smithsonian Museum of Natural History's Botany department remarked, "carrion beetles and other pollinators from its native Sumatra are attracted to the smell....These beetles usually lay their eggs in rotting animals, so this plant pretends to be a dead animal" (CNN 2005).

Clearly, this plant should make people stay way from the smell, if it smells as rancid as reported. However, Kress also commented that the plant and its smell were attracting human visitors in the thousands, daily. If the plant mimics the odor of a dead animal well enough to attract insects that lay their eggs in dead animals, then why are humans attracted to the plant? Furthermore, since there is a plant that grows like this one and gives off a similar smell to a rotting corpse, then why isn't there a mortuary ritual for these kinds of flowers? The answer is that the smell of a dead body probably has little to do with the performance of mortuary rituals. In other words, as the empirical evidence seems to imply, mortuary rituals are not specifically tailored to dispose of the corpse because of their odor (as a dangerous pathogen).

As Axel (2006) argues from experimental research, humans apparently are capable of differentiating between ten-thousand or more different scents that are received in the posterior of the nose, in what is called the olfactory epithelium. The olfactory epithelium then sends a variety of "neural messages" via the olfactory bulb (behind the nose), which are routed to either the neocortex (where higher level thinking is found) or to more ancestral parts of the brain that instigate actions like fight or flight. However, only sexual smells are sent to the more ancestral regions such as the "limbic system," meaning the majority of smells are processed by mental systems in the neocortex of the brain. If the smell of a corpse was processed by the olfactory epithelium, then it would go by way of the neo-cortex first and then to the limbic region of the brain.

This molecular evidence might suggest that highly complex thinking is involved in the processing of dangerous pathogens involved in smell, not an unconscious, reflexive type mechanism; therefore, if the scent of a corpse or dead animal did, in fact, trigger such disgust reflexes (activating a contagion-avoidance system), it would be processed in the neocortex first and then the limbic system. That is unless the sense of smell toward dead bodies stimulates the same neural messages as sexual smells. This is most likely not the case. Insomuch as the processing of smell may inform science of the compulsion towards ritual behavior towards dead bodies, the body does seem to trigger, or get tagged by a "biological warning system" (BWS) causing humans to behave as if corpses, and objects or places associated with dead bodies, were contagious and/or disgusting. Dead bodies appear to get this tag, even though empirical evidence seems to suggest smell plays very little role in the stimulation of a biological warning system for contagion-avoidance toward dead bodies.

So, disposal of corpses does not appear to be adaptive for the reason that dead bodies produce toxic smells that might harm humans.[3]

Despite this, Boyer's initial claim about the triggering of specific cognitive systems bequeathed by evolution is one that should be exploited. So a good question to pose now is: is there an evolutionarily viable alternative to the explanation I have attempted to refute above? Though Boyer argues that the mental systems involved in the ritualized disposal of dead bodies are adaptions from natural selection—evolution—clearly the actual compulsion to handle dead bodies in special ways and the generation of rich counterintuitive inferences about them is a by-product of the mental system's natural functional purpose.

Summary

In Chapter Seven, I raise the question of the evolutionary reasons for the ritualized disposal of dead bodies. If this behavior is so widespread and natural, then according to evolutionary theory, there should be selective reasons for it. After all, according to Dawinian theory, organisms adapt to their environment to survive and replicate the species. What is it then that benefits humans in performing ritualized disposal? Pascal Boyer suggests that the answer to this problem is not to be found in the behavior itself, but in several mental systems that were selected for in the course of human evolution, many of which are meant to process information about social relationships concerning agents.

Boyer names five such systems: Animacy, Theory of Mind, Hyperactive Agency Detection Device (HADD), Person-file, and Contagion-Avoidance. All of these important systems evolved in humans to handle specific important mental tasks for survival. Boyer and Steven Mithen conclude that due to a small but significant change (adaptation) in the "fluidity" of the *Homo sapiens*

---

[3] See McCorkle (*forthcoming –a*) for an argument against the corpses' smell as a factor in regard to ritualized disposal. I claim that the dead body activates multiple mental systems that cause ritualized disposal, by individuals and groups. Smell, I argue, may be a factor due to individuals involved in the mortuary behavior(s) producing various chemicals (i.e., pheromones), that others in the group process in the limbic system, where sexual odors are managed (see Axel 2006). Moreover, these pheromones may produce sexual and predatory (symbolic and non-symbolic) behaviors by the mortuary participants towards the cadaver and themselves, as documented by anthropologists (see especially Bloch & Parry 1982; Bloch 1991; Metcalf & Huntington 1991).

cognitive architecture over the last several hundred thousand years, these systems function as an aggregate whole, in other words they work together to solve problems in the human environment. Although there are significant reasons for handling corpses carefully, and social groups utilize salient cultural devices (e.g., disgust, taboo, prohibitions, and rituals) to categorize and transform the dead, the biological threat (e.g., smell, disease) to the living is extremely marginal to the risks involved in handling dead bodies.

I (along with Boyer and others) argue that our understanding of dead bodies is not so much about the physical corpse and the biological danger it intuitively represents, but about the ways in which the aggregate mental systems—meant to handle living, moving agents—process biologically dead "people." In summary, humans adapted specialized mental systems to handle living people and to process complex social arrangements; it is merely a by-product of these systems that humans perform ritualized behaviors to dead bodies and produce rich counterintuitive inferences about the corpses. Furthermore, social groups have culturally constrained these behaviors, because dead bodies appear frequently throughout human history.

Part Four

FROM CORPSE TO CONCEPT

Chapter Eight

Corpse, Concept, and Contagion Triggers

Psychotic persons do not respond to dead bodies in the same way as normal persons. Extreme psychotics are primarily concerned with *objectifying* their victim.[1] They sometimes wear parts of the body, keep the corpse or parts near them, or consume the body. This extreme objectification of the victim by the psychotic is often reported as involving the transfer of the victim's 'essence' to the psychotic. Nowhere is this more apparent than in the case of serial killer Jeffrey Dahmer.

In interviews (MSNBC 2005 (replay)) after his arrest, Dahmer responded that he was driven to cannibalism because he, "wanted to have the victims under his complete control." Dahmer claimed that by eating his victim's body parts and internal organs, "it made me *feel* they were a permanent part of me" (*emphasis added*). Whatever his purported reasons, Dahmer engaged in various acts of handling, storing, and displaying the remainder of non-digested corpses; Dahmer moved them around in different places and in different ways. What is interesting here is that Dahmer, as well as other psychotic serial killers, did not *dispose of* the bodies.[2]

Interestingly enough, fMRI (*functional Magnetic Resonance Imaging*) experiments with serial killers have shown that the limbic system in these extreme

---

[1] As Meloy (1988) defines this characteristic as "a process in which affective and ideational components of the individual are attributed to another, while at the same time the other actual person is controlled, or attempted to be controlled. Projective identification, by necessity, implies both false attribution and object control. [This]...[involves] repetitive simulations, and it is closely tied to incorporative and expulsive libidinal themes....Projective identification may mobilize anxiety and discomfort during the psychopathic process" (p. 141).

[2] It could be argued that technically he did dispose of the bits he consumed. However, across cultures (non-symbolic) cannibalism is extremely rare and not a universal tendency of the sort with which we are concerned here.

psychotics does not "light up" (neural activity detected by a blood oxygen level) (Belliveau, Rosen, et al. 1990; Belliveau, Kennedy et al. 1991; Ogawa et al. 1990a; Ogawa et al. 1990b; Ogawa et al. 1992; Ogawa et al. 1993) in the same way it does in normal subjects when an emotional stimulus (e.g., death, fear, anxiety) is introduced (Hare 1999).[3] Studies done by Robert Hare and his colleagues (Kiehl et al. 2001) using functional Magnetic Resonance Imaging (fMRI) have shown that subjects with high scores for Psychoticism (or Tough-mindedness) on the Eysenck personality scale (+P/TM) (H. J. Eysenck 1992) display little, if any, activity in the limbic system. Hare et al. interpreted this as psychotics having significantly low emotional responses in anxiety experiments. In the same studies, fMRI scans of subjects with low Psychoticism scores (normal subjects) displayed significantly greater amounts of neural activity (in the limbic region), which Hare et al. interpreted as a high emotional response. This fits with what is known about psychopathic serial killers, for example, who do not exhibit high emotional responses to dead bodies, i.e., Dahmer, Bundy, Gacy, BTK etc. (Reid 1986).[4]

Based on Hare's studies and the literature describing serial killer behavior, one would expect persons with a low Psychoticism score to have high emotional responses (i.e., scored by analyzing fMRI scans) when exposed to some sort of corpse stimulus and those with a high Psychoticism score would have a lower emotional response.[5] These tests may help us to understand those mechanisms that inform our responses to and behavior toward dead bodies.

Currently, the comparative results between the Eysenck personality inventory (EPQ-R) and the "Big Five School Place" inventory suggests that high Psychoticism/Tough-mindedness scores in *normal* subjects (normal popula-

---

[3] In another set of experiments, Hare used different dictionary terms that used no emotional tags such as "Paper." He then tested concepts like "Death" that were terms tagged with an emotional meaning. He used an EEG machine to measure the responses. The psychopath "responded to the emotionally tagged words as neutral" (Hare 1999, pp. 129–30).

[4] In fact, in experiments by Eysenck and others, the extreme psychotic may actually be drawn to high extraversion (sensory bombardment) because of a neurological state, as identified by "low levels of cortical arousal," even in higher "thrill seeking" situations (Meloy 1988, pp. 34–36).

[5] Miller clearly notes that Rozin's claims concerning disgust and contagion are that "Core Disgust" (in response to various stimuli including dead bodies) "is a cognitively sophisticated *emotion*" based upon evolutionary "reminders" of a human's animal past (Miller 1997, p. 6) (my italics).

tion) on the Eysenck EPQ-R are found within several traits in the Big Five (e.g., Neuroticism, Extraversion, Originality, Accommodation, and Consolidation),(Howard & Howard 2006; Zuckerman 1993, pp. 757-768). The Psychoticism/Tough-mindedness (P/TM) trait of the Eysenck scale is split into multiple traits in the Big Five. As a result there is a wide variation in continuum scores between the two scales. So, in the Big Five scale *Neuroticism* (i.e., the need for stability), *Extraversion* (i.e., the attraction to sensory stimulation), or *Originality* (i.e., imagination, cleverness) might be extremely high while in the Eysenck scale mainly Psychoticism will be high, though there is a direct correlation between Psychoticism and Extraversion since the P/TM scale was built upon the Extraversion scale in Eysenck's model (e.g., H. J. Eysenck & Eysenck, Sybil B. G. 1994, pp. 1, 4-5; Meloy 1988, p. 34).

There has also been a direct correlation between *Extraversion* and *Psychoticism* in experimental research (Meloy 1988, pp. 33-37, 111). It appears that individuals with high P/TM are attracted to high levels of sensory stimulation in order to "compensate for lower levels of cortical arousal" (p. 111). Moreover, these wide differences in scores suggest that normal subjects with scores on the high end of the normal P/TM spectrum tend to be preoccupied with responses to other agents and perceived agency. These subjects have scores on the Big Five scale that reflect a preoccupation with other agents, their actions, and complex thinking about agents and actions—dimensions of the scale that are designed to understand how well subjects respond to other agents and environments (Howard 2000).

The significance of these claims about pathological responses to dead bodies can best be evaluated by a set of experimental studies that I performed in the spring of 2006.

Experiments and Correlations

Subjects. Seventy-eight subjects (N=78) recruited from (two) liberal arts introduction courses at a North American (Southeast) state university participated. They ranged in age from 18 to 54 years old, with a mean age of 21.7 years and a median age of 20. Forty-one were female, thirty-seven male. Participants were from a range of different religious denominations including Christians (e.g., Protestant, Catholic, and Greek Orthodox), Muslims (Sunni and Shi'a), Bud-

dhists, Jews, Hindus, and indigenous African traditions. The majority, however, were Protestant Christians from North America. All the subjects were
from a wide variety of majors within a liberal arts curriculum.

Materials. The Eysenck Personality Inventory-Revised (EPQ-R) measuring
Psychoticism/Tough-mindedness (P/TM), Extraversion (E), Neuroticism (N),
and Lie (L); the Big Five "School Place" 2.0 instrument measuring Need for
stability/Neuroticism (N), Extraversion (E), Originality (O), Accommodation
(A), and Consolidation (C) plus twenty-four sub-traits; the Haidt, Rozin, and
McCauley "Disgust" inventory; a series of six (6) vignettes (de-
signed/constructed by McCorkle called The DIG 5).

The vignettes were as follows:

Vignette 1: John and Terrie met in college and became fast friends. After they
graduated they both moved to a big city nearby. Eventually they fell in love
and married. After several years together, children, and a nice house, John became very sick all of a sudden. Before John or Terrie knew what was making
John ill, he died.

Vignette 2: Fran and Taylor were recently married. They have been looking
for their first house to buy together. However, most of the houses have been
too expensive for them to purchase. Their real estate agent called them today
to show them a house that has recently come onto the market. It is in a nice
neighborhood and, price-wise, is within their budget. They met with the real
estate agent and viewed the house. They are really excited about the house;
however, they wonder why it is so inexpensive.

Vignette 3: You graduated from college and have decided to enroll into medical school to become a doctor. You are smart but more importantly you have
worked very hard to get to this level. You are also outgoing and enjoy doing
activities that are not class related. The first class you are required to take this
semester is called *Gross Anatomy*. The class is from 11:30am till 3pm Monday
through Friday. This class covers the basic graduate skills to understand the

human body. You are not sure what to expect but look forward to the challenge of medical school.

Vignette 4: You recently went on a trip to the beach. This trip was just what you needed to relax. One day while you were out there weren't that many people on the beach. So, you decided to take a book and a drink/food cooler and get some sun. However, after about thirty minutes out on the beach you encountered a drowning victim. There is no one else around.

Vignette 5: You recently went on a vacation to an exotic island. This trip was just what you needed to relax. One day you were out on a tour of several ancient ruins. The locals dated them to around the seventeenth century CE. There were a great number of caves. They had all kinds of strange writing and statues on the outside of them. You decide to explore one of the caves.

Vignette 6: In a hundred words or less, please describe your first experience with a dead body. Try to be as precise as possible about what happened and how you felt.

Procedure. Participants were told nothing about the purpose of the study. They recorded their age, date of birth, and sex on the response sheets. The participants took each of the three inventory scales (Eysenck, Big Five, and Disgust). The participants were then asked to respond to questions about each of the vignettes (206 total) on a 5 point "Likert" scale (-2, -1, 0, 1, 2) (Likert 1932) (Vig. 1 (31), Vig. 2 (51), Vig. 3 (31), Vig. 4 (31), Vig. 5 (31), and Vig. 6 (31)). The inventory scales and the vignettes were taken over a two month period.

The vignette questions were specifically designed to correlate with Pascal Boyer's five systems (e.g., Animacy, Intuitive Psychology, Person-file, Predation, and Contagion systems) discussed in Chapter Six of *Religion Explained* (Boyer 2001, pp. 203-28). Vignettes 1 through 5 were hypothetical scenarios with questions designed to measure a subject's interaction with a dead body at various stages in decomposition (wet/dry). In addition questions in vignettes one through five measured the context in which subjects encountered a corpse. Vignette six's questions measured the subjects first "remembered" encounter with a dead body.

Vignette Analysis 1

1. I did item analyses in order to determine which of my items (in the six vignettes) failed to discriminate, i.e., they tended to elicit a near universal response. These questions were stricken from further analysis. They didn't measure anything (meaning 80% or more subjects responded with the same categorical response (–2 and –1), (0), or (+1 and +2).

2. I performed a Cronbach's alpha (α) analyses in order to determine if the items designed to measure a particular "system" in fact were all measuring the same thing, with the result of eliminating items unrelated to the system.

Questions and systems

Here I define the five mental systems (see also the Appendix for detailed vignette questions and significant correlations).

System 1 – Animacy system

Animacy is the awareness that we have to distinguish between things that have purposeful movement and things that don't. Typically the Animacy system would be stimulated by a human, animal, or plant. However, it is possible for non-agents like a machine (windmill), tool (computer), or an element (fire, water, rock) (i.e., rock falls down the cliff into the street) to stimulate the Animacy system. Furthermore, lack of movement may also stimulate the Animacy system, such as an animal that is not moving, or the sudden lack of movement of an object (computer screen freezes up while watching a movie). The Animacy system is a crucial system to distinguish between agents and objects.

System 2 - Predation/HADD system

The *Hyperactive Agency Detection Device* (HADD) or Predation system is stimulated by the hypersensitivity to not only movement, but the awareness of agency in the near vicinity. If the bush wiggles, humans are predisposed to trigger HADD and explain what the agent is and if it is potentially dangerous (as in a predatory awareness system). This hypersensitivity is set for identification of potential predator/prey identification and may generate many false positives. A good example would be in horror movies where a sound or movement may generate a sense of fight or flight and/or heightened emotional anxiety toward the stimuli. This can be seen especially if someone were to watch a horror movie in an old, dark house by oneself at night. Accordingly, hypersensitivity might cause one to become scared and make many false positives about potential agents in or around the house. "The house goes bump in the night."

System 3 – Intuitive psychology system (Theory of Mind)

The *Theory of Mind* module is an inferential psychological system about another agent's (or sometimes object's) feelings, emotions, or thoughts. Example: "Lucy thinks the world is out to get her," or "I know what you are feeling." Many times we infer things about an animal's thoughts. Example: "Roscoe is so happy to see me today," or "Tinkerbell loves her doggie bone." Even objects seem to trigger the ToM system on occasion. Example: "The computer hates me. That is why it isn't working for me today." Humans appear to be proficient from four to six levels of theory of mind.

System 4 – Person-file system

The *Person-file* system is the collection of data about an agent over a span of time (hours, days, weeks, and/or years). The Person-file system is triggered as a mental mechanism for social relationships. Example: "Leanne gossips about everyone; therefore, if I want to keep a secret I better not tell Leanne." Person-file is important as a mental storage house where data on individuals or groups is kept until needed for utility. The death of a loved one or a favorite pet might also stimulate such a system. Example: "Remember that time Roscoe dove out into the lake and chased the ducks around," or at a funeral, "Billy was always a stand-up guy, he always was there for his friends in time of need."

System 5 – Contagion-avoidance system

The *Contagion-avoidance* system is stimulated by the awareness of dangerous pathogens in the environment that trigger reflexes such as disgust. This reflex is designed to protect us from potential harm by toxins or dangerous biological/chemical stimuli. Example: "Don't go to the bathroom here, the toilet seat looks like it hasn't been cleaned, EVER!" The contagion/disgust system is also related to things that come into contact with potential environmental hazards. Example: "I don't want to sleep in that bed where Lucy has been sick all week long, even though the room, sheets, and pillowcases have been cleaned. The bed is still contagious from her." This system might also be triggered by potential hazards that are quite negligible to the risk of contact. Example: "Don't shake a person's hand who has AIDS or cancer, because you might get it from them." As a result, this system does not have to be triggered by a "real" threat, but might also be triggered by an imagined one as well. The Contagion-avoidance system may in fact be directly related to ontological violations concerning Agency/Object classification.

Predictions. Participants' P/TM scores will be inversely proportional to their disgust towards dead bodies and their empathy toward the corpse (Person-file) as represented in their scores on vignettes 1–6.

Results. There was a continuum based upon the subjects and their P/TM scores. The (raw) mean of the group was (8.05), the median was (8.0), and the standard deviation (SD) was (3.17). This was higher than the general populace (Mean/SD=5.72/3.21 for males and Mean/SD=4.61/2.97 for females) (H. J. Eysenck, Eysenck, Sybil B. G. 1994).[6]

---

[6] I would like to thank Professor Noel Sheehy (formerly the Head of the School of Psychology at Queen's University, Belfast and now at the University of Liverpool) for his generous input early on in this research. Noel suggested that I might study the Psychoticism/Tough-mindedness of student populations instead of clinical or prison populations, since I was interested in the ritualized disposal of dead bodies as normal behavior.

Vignette Analysis 2

3. I determined the means and standard deviations of the five systems and
    the traits to:
        a. establish scoring formulas for the five systems, and
        b. demonstrate whether or not (using established trait norms) the
        sample was biased/representative of the world at large (see *Table* 8.1
        and 8.2).
Note: the means are all near 50 (on a hundred point scale) and within a standard deviation (+ or -) of the mean. These means and standard deviations help me establish standardized scores from raw scores, so that I could analyze between systems and instruments.

Table 8.1 Descriptive Statistics for Five Mental Systems

Mental Systems	N	Mean	*Std. Dev*
Animacy	43	49.48	10.06
Predation	43	50.19	10.27
Intuitive Psychology	43	50.42	9.64
Person-file	43	49.88	9.24
Contagion	43	49.08	10.29

Table 8.2 Descriptive Statistics for Big Five "School Place" 2.0 Traits

Personality Traits	N	Mean	Std. Dev
N (Need for Stability)	43	48.33	7.32
E (Extraversion)	43	50.12	5.83
O (Originality)	43	50	8.34
A (Accommodation)	43	53.40	7.88
CS (Consolidation)	43	52.14	5.93
N1 (Worry)	43	49.44	9.27
N2 (Temper)	43	46.28	11.07
N3 (Outlook)	43	48.91	9.21
N4 (Coping Level)	43	47.77	8.69
E1 (Approach Level)	43	46.28	10.61
E2 (Group Orientation)	43	51.81	9.89
E3 (Pace)	43	49.30	9.93

Table 8.2 continued			
E4 (Leadership)	43	49.93	8.98
E5 (Trust)	43	52.33	10.95
E6 (Tact)	43	51.67	9.17
O1 (Imagination)	43	46.30	11.64
O2 (Range of Interests)	43	51.21	10.01
O3 (Innovation)	43	51.26	9.82
O4 (Zoom Scale)	43	50.16	9.56
A1 (Service)	43	52	9.56
A2 (Compliance)	43	52.35	9.07
A3 (Humility)	43	53.86	9.83
A4 (Speak Out Level)	43	52.19	11.48
A5 (Timidness)	43	54.07	9.68
C1 (Thoroughness)	43	51.95	9.13
C2 (Structure)	43	53.47	9.87
C3 (Ambition)	43	50.37	7.64
C4 (Concentration)	43	50.30	9.21
C5 (Methodicalness)	43	54.19	8.52

4. I did simple correlation analyses to determine:

   a. whether the five systems were independent of each other (see *Table 8.3*), and

   b. whether each of the five systems were systematically related to behavioral traits (see *Tables 8.5, 8.6,* and *8.7*).

Table 8.3 Correlation of Five Mental Systems

N=57	Animacy	Predation	Intuitive Psychology	Person-file	Contagion
Animacy System	1	0.07	**0.92**	**0.55**	**0.71**
Predation System	0.07	1	0.02	**0.61**	0.11
Intuitive Psychology	**0.92**	–0.02	1	**0.49**	**0.56**
Person-File System	**0.55**	**0.61**	**0.49**	1	**0.36**
Contagion System	**0.71**	0.11	**0.56**	**0.36**	1

Bold is significant at the 0.01 level

c. I performed a simple correlation on the Haidt, McCauley, and Rozin "Disgust" inventory to other systems and P/TM (see *Table* 8.4).

Table 8.4 Correlation with Haidt et al. "Disgust" Inventory

N=43	Animacy	Intuitive Psychology	Contagion	P/TM
H/R/M Disgust	−.55	−.45	−.51	−.39

Bold Significance is .01

Therefore, P/TM subjects appeared to score proportionally to the Animacy system and the Intuitive Psychology system, but scores were inversely proportional to their disgust and contagion-avoidance (negative = avoidance of) (seen again in *Table* 8.4).

d. Normal Subject Group (see *Table* 8.5).

Table 8.5 Normal Populace in EPQ-R scale

N=57	P/TM	Extraversion	Neuroticism	*Lie*
Animacy	.20	.14	−.07	.05
Predation	−.14	.17	**.40****	.06
Intuitive Psychology	.13	.12	−.13	.10
Person-file	−.11	.35*	.20	.20
Contagion-avoidance	.12	−.06	−.15	-.03
Disgust	−.39			

Significance * = .05 and ** .01

e. Extremes Representing Pathological Groups P/TM (less than or equal to 3 and more than or equal to 12 on the raw EPQ-R scale) (see *Table* 8.6).

Table 8.6 Extreme Scores Representing Pathological Groups

N=9	P/TM
Animacy	.09
Predation	**–.60**
Intuitive Psychology	.06
Person-file	**–.40**
Contagion-avoidance	–.10
Disgust	**–.64**

5. I performed a *multiple regression analysis* to determine whether a group of traits (on the Big Five "School Place" 2.0) used together were associated with a particular system more strongly than any of the single traits taken alone (see *Table* 8.7).

Table 8.7 Multiple Regression Analysis between Mental Systems and Big Five "School Place" 2.0

Dependent Variables	Prediction Variables	*r*
Animacy System	A1, O1, E2, O4, O3, E5, O2, E, O	0.72
Predation System	E5, N1	0.49
Intuitive Psychology system	A1, O1, E2, O4, O3, E5, O2, E, O	0.71
Person–file System	A1, A3, E2, O, E5, E, E6, O4, O2	0.67
Contagion–Avoidance System	O2, N4, O	0.45

Discussion

According to the results from the five major analyses performed, the evidence seems to imply that high P/TM subjects score higher in responses to dead bodies on systems specifically activated by Animacy and Intuitive Psychology. However, high P/TM subjects score extremely low in response to systems activated by corpse stimuli such as Disgust and Person-file system. Low P/TM subjects appear to score the inverse of the High P/TM subjects. Normal subjects appear to score those systems more toward the means. In other words, the closer the subject is to the means on P/TM, the less discrepancy between sys-tems in extreme high or low scores.

This would seem to proffer evidence that P/TM (along with other traits) is a possible index for variation between systems activated by corpse stimuli. In addition, *disgust* towards dead bodies by subjects appears not to be stimulated as "turned on, turned off," but turned on or off according to various grades. In other words, these systems appear to have variable complex psychological activations rather than simply on/off activations. This evidence seems to imply that certain personality traits (e.g., Psychoticism/Tough-mindedness, Extraver-sion, Neuroticism, and Originality and various sub-traits) are highly reliable in predicting how a subject will respond to corpse stimuli. This suggests evidence to support that a cognitive model of the mind may inform our mental repre-sentation systems concerning dead bodies and, also, our subsequent cultural behavior in the processing of these mental representations.

Examples

For example, in Vignette number 5 subjects were given a hypothetical scenario based upon a vacation to an exotic island where they accidentally stumbled upon an ancient burial cave/tomb holding several skeletons aged approxi-mately three-hundred years.[7] They were then asked to respond to a series of 31 questions.

Subject no. 71 in the study measured the highest on the Eysenck P/TM scale (P/TM=18). This was more than three times higher than the mean for the general populace and more than twice the mean of the subject's group. Subjects no. 40, 44, and 62 were then chosen because they had the lowest scores on the Eysenck P/TM scale (P/TM= 2, 2, and 2 respectively). Subjects 40, 44, and 62 were almost one fourth the average for the P/TM scale of their peer group (they represented the extremes for the group). After certain pre-liminary criteria were eliminated from the vignettes (Questions 1, 2, 10, and 21 were eliminated because over 80% of the subjects scored in the same Likert range, -2 and -1, 0, and +1 and +2. They did not appear to measure any dif-

---

[7] Several of the other vignettes tested what might be deemed "wet" corpses. See, specifically Bloch & Parry (1982). I purposely used vignettes that would test varying degrees of wet and dry corpses to test the difference between the age of a corpse and the reaction to them by subjects.

ferences in attitudes towards those questions), subjects 40, 44, and 62 scored the same range on questions 8, 12, 14, 23, and 30. Subject no. 71 scored differently on all of these questions (8, 12, 14, 23, and 30). The questions were as follows:

Vignette No. 5

8. You don't mind looking at the skeleton even though it still appears to look at you?

12. You think that the skeleton's spirit is watching what you do in the cave/tomb?

14. You want to wash your clothes as soon as possible after handling the skeleton?

23. You think skeletons are disgusting, but not infectious?

30. You think that others might find taking a questionnaire like this uncomfortable to them?

On many of the 31 questions from Vignette No. 5, subject 71 (P/TM=18) scored responses that might be seen as a lack of empathy supporting the main hypothesis; however, on question No. 8 subject 71 scored high, while the other (low P/TM) subjects did not. Subject 71 appeared not to be bothered by dead skeletons or their biological contamination; however, when the skeleton appeared to be looking back (imagined), subject 71 reversed scores with the others. Even more interesting was subject no. 71's low response (1) in question No. 12. This subject did not think that the skeleton's spirit was watching over them. In addition, Subject no. 71 scored very low in responses to handling dead skeletons throughout the vignette, including skeletons that either were explicitly infectious or died of an infectious disease (question no. 23, 25). In question no. 14, subject no. 71 did not feel compelled to wash his or her clothes or body after handling the skeleton. Subjects 40, 44, and 62 scored in the opposite direction from subject no. 71 on these questions.

In a related correlation, these same subjects were given the Haidt, McCauley, and Rozin "Disgust" inventory (Haidt et al. 1993). These same low P/TM and high P/TM subjects scored in the mid-range of this disgust inventory (74–75) (Haidt 1993). After looking at the questions that each subject scored high for disgust, it became rather apparent that dead bodies and parts were scored high by the low P/TM subjects and low for disgust by the high P/TM subject. In addition, the questions that the high P/TM subject scored high and were scored low by the low P/TM subjects for disgust, were topics pertaining to cleanliness and bodily fluids. In summary, things that were biological contaminants (perceived or real) were highly disgusting to the subject with high P/TM, though he or she was not bothered by dead bodies or parts. In addition, dead bodies and parts did not appear to trigger the same types of cognitive warning systems as bodily fluids and cleanliness; therefore, the subject that scored as not disgusted by the contagiousness of a dead body did so because *the body was not perceived as a biological threat to the subject like other biological hazards.*

Once again, in Vignette number five on the same questions as posed earlier, two subjects (59, 67) closer toward the mean (P/TM = 6, 8 respectively) (N=6) were added to this specific table. These subjects answered in the midrange on the above questions (8, 12, 14, 23, and 30) (see *Graph* 8.1). This suggests a strong correlation between the P/TM scale and responses to dead bodies and the lack of disgust towards them based upon this sample.

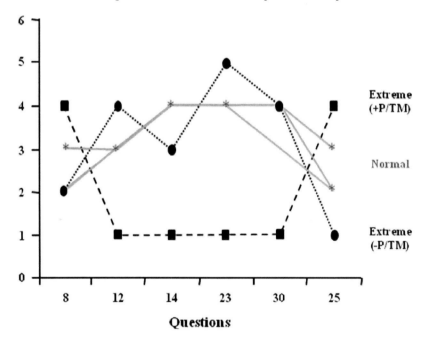

Graph 8.1 Vignette No. 5 with Question No. 25 Added

Subjects with high P/TM scored very low with regard to their reactions to dead bodies (especially disgust; they did not seem to be bothered by any potential biological contamination concerning dead bodies: question no. 14, 23), high on questions about intuitive psychology (question no. 8), and extremely low on questions that correlated with the Person-file system (specifically they scored low in empathy to other individual corpses as people).   Those subjects with low P/TM scored high on disgust toward dead bodies, low on questions about intuitive psychology, and high on Person-file questions.

These results correlate with current behavioral research on extreme psychotics. Robert Hare has created a *Psychopathy Checklist* (Hare 1999) that categorizes and scores psychopathology by closely related behavioral traits. These traits include "glib and superficial, egocentric and grandiose, lack of empathy, deceitful and manipulative, shallow emotions, impulsive, poor behavioral controls, need for excitement, lack of responsibility, early behavior problems and adult antisocial behavior" (Hare 1999, 69–70).

In other words, the higher the Psychoticism scores then (1) the less empathy toward other individuals (i.e., Person-file) (see also, Meloy 1988, p. 114) and (2) the less disgust reaction (contagion/contamination) toward dead bodies. Low P/TM subjects are extremely motivated by Disgust and Person-file systems in response to dead bodies, but not hypersensitive to the agency and related systems as seen in this model. In addition, a normal population of subjects would operate on a continuum based upon their P/TM (or Big Five) scores where the systems would be processed on a variable continuum in closer relation to each other.

Why do psychotics respond differently to dead bodies?

The reason that extremely high P/TM subjects are not disgusted by dead bodies and feel little empathy towards other individuals, while low P/TM subjects score in the opposite directions on the continuum (both representing the pathological group), is explained best by a breakdown in the cognitive fluidity of Mithen's "Swiss army knife" theory (1996) (i.e., where specialized systems developed into a complex, general purpose system). Normal populations do exhibit varied responses to corpse stimuli; however, *they do so within a close range, and, furthermore they do not "cut off" certain systems entirely such as the*

High/Low P/TM subjects did. This may be helpful for understanding why existing theories from psychopathology have been unable to account for psychotic behavior.

Recent theories have revolved around two specific arguments; the sociobiological argument where extreme psychotics never achieve full mature mental development, resulting in a "reptilian" sense of predatory and sexual propriety. In this theory the world literally revolves around the psychotic and their quest to reproduce with as many mates as possible, unlike normal human populations, where mate selection is also an economic activity (Hare 1999, pp. 166-67). Reproduction is carefully selected by normal populations of humans for successful resource allocation (to the offspring). The psychotic, however, operates on a system where little developmental parenting and resource allocation is given to the offspring, resembling "reptilian" behavior (Meloy 1988, pp. 69-74) where the extreme psychotic is driven to procreate as much as possible, siring multiple offspring to offset the lack of attention given by the psychotic to the offspring.[8] Apparently, this behavior can be directly seen in male and female populations of extreme P/TM subjects (167-68). Nevertheless according to research by experts in Psychopathology (Hare 1999, pp. 166-69), sociobiological explanations do not appear sufficient to explain the diverse group of behavioral traits in extreme psychotics.

The second theory has resulted in observations that some extreme psychotics have frontal lobe damage (i.e., the part of the brain associated with order and highly complex mental function) (Damasio et al. 1990), either lack of development of this region of the brain (Kegan 1986) or neurological failure in this region (Hoffman et al. 1987). However, recently scientists researching these claims have found these notions to be unable to explain the majority of psychopathological behavior (Hare 1999, pp. 169-70). Therefore, though some psychotics have damage or problems with this region of the brain, the

---

[8] The psychotic may not be consciously aware of their behavior as a "mating strategy." In fact, one of the key problems with this theory is that all of the same predatory traits (e.g., extraversion, sexual encounters, manipulation, and objectification) are consistent with psychopathology as a whole. Most psychotics do not engage in violent predatory behavior involving sexual crimes. This problem may be best explained by the notion that psychopathology, or Psychoticism is not one illness, but many under the rubric of similar behavioral traits (Hare 1999, p. 74).

neurological (brain) research does not support this as a universal theory of psychopathology either.[9]

My correlation studies together with Mithen's description of the "Swiss army knife" model for the evolution of the *Homo sapiens* mind and Boyer's "Hazard-Precaution" model, seem to provide a start to a more compelling account of psychopathology with regard to dead bodies, the variation of responses to dead bodies in normal populations, and the tendency for normal populations to engage in religious ritualized disposal of dead bodies, seen here, in this EQ (i.e., Emotional Quotient) model for a normal population (see *Figure* 8.1):

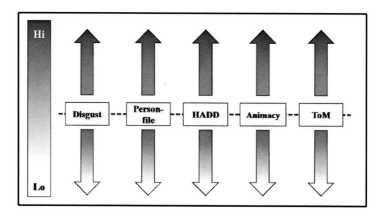

Figure 8.1 Normal Population Scores in Response to Dead Bodies

According to the EQ (emotional quotient) model above, normal subjects have variable settings of the five systems, like an Equalizer on a stereo system. In a response to dead bodies, some individuals EQ jazz settings, some EQ rock settings, and some subjects EQ classical settings (an analogy). All of these are normal settings for the activation of Boyer's five systems. Unlike the pathological group, they are in fact probably closer to each other than the high/low

---

[9] See Baron-Cohen (1997) for an overview of the current research on cognitive pathology involving Theory of Mind in autistic individuals. Further studies on Autism, Asperger syndrome, and psychopathology may produce better models for the cognitive architecture of human minds, since they reveal dysfunctions of "normal" mental capacities and processes.

EQ of the extreme groups. Their cognitive systems are fluid, while pathological groups appear not to have a fully fluid cognitive mental architecture.

Some problems with the P/TM scale

The Psychoticism trait measured well with the extremes. The P/TM trait (N=9) had strong negative loadings on the Predation system (-.60), moderate negative loadings on the Person-file system (-.40) and strong negative loadings on the Haidt/Rozin/McCauley "Disgust" inventory (-.64); however, when the total population was analyzed (N=57), the P/TM lost its power in the Predation system (-.14), the Person-file system (-.11), and in the Haidt, Rozin, and McCauley "Disgust" inventory (-.39). There were also strong correlations between Eysenck's P/TM and E (Extraversion) with strong loadings in Person-file (.64) and moderate loadings in the Haidt, Rozin, and McCauley "Disgust" inventory (.41); however, there were no significant loadings for Predation (.27). In addition, in the larger group (N=57) P/TM had negative loadings on N1: worry (-.34) and C2: Organization (-.38) that were significant (.05).

This expands on the previous predictions of P/TM in regard to dead bodies. High P/TM subjects are not disgusted toward dead bodies and feel little empathy for other individuals. Apparently, they are not hypersensitive to Predation, but this may be because they appear to be "chaotic" or "erratic" in their behavior (i.e. they don't organize, plan and/or worry about their day to day activities, resulting in a "live by the moment" lifestyle). They simply might not notice a corpse, or pay very little attention to it. If a person died in front of them they might just keep walking because they were on their way to get food or go shopping. High P/TM subjects, however, are attracted to sensory bombardment; so, they might actually hang around a dead body if there were a certain amount of sensory stimulation involved that was indirectly related to the corpse. They would probably not feel the need to perform any kind of disposal action in a ritualized way. (see *Figure* 8.2). Notice that high P/TM subjects who are high in E (Extraversion) are not disturbed by disgust or predation, nor do they find empathy for other individuals (i.e., Person-file).

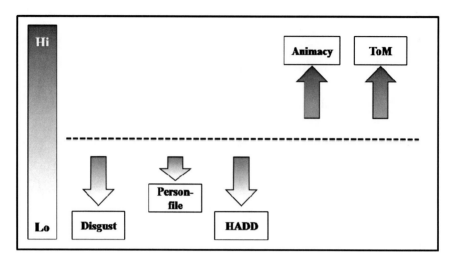

Figure 8.2 + (High) Psychoticism/Tough-Mindedness Scores in Response to Dead Bodies

Low P/TM subjects might be incredibly sensitive to corpse stimuli. They might become emotional just hearing about death or dead bodies. Even the thought of a dead body might also make them sick with disgust. They would be extremely sensitive to anything that even came in contact with a dead body, and would probably refuse to touch anything associated with it (e.g., clothes, jewelry, and sleeping in the bed or house of a dead person). They would probably avoid hospitals like the plague. Moreover, they might be extremely introverted (and there is a direct negative correlation between the trait E and disgust and contagion), especially when it comes to grieving over a dead body. They might also be the type of person who jumps at the slightest thing, hears movement in the house when they are all alone (Predation), and possibly takes great care to handle ceremonies in the proper way (see *Figure* 8.3).

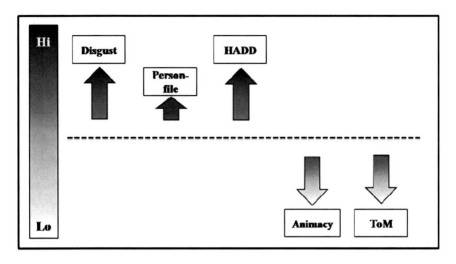

Figure 8.3 - (Low) Psychoticism/Tough-Mindedness Scores in Response to Dead Bodies

So, to sum up, high P/TM individuals would not feel the need to dispose of a dead body but might (for a desire for sensory stimulation) touch it, eat it but could otherwise ignore it due to a lack of disgust and empathy. Low P/TM individuals would have a great need to dispose of the body but would have to do so in a way that would satisfy the constraints imposed by their high degree of empathy. Both groups are representative of, at best, a dysfunctional sample and at worst a pathological sample.

Explanations

There are several probable reasons for the discrepancy between the extremes and the whole in the above analysis. First, the Eysenck EPQ–R was originally designed and tested for pathological populations (especially prison populations of psychotics) (H. J. Eysenck 1992; H. J. Eysenck & Eysenck, Sybil B. G. 1994, pp. 1-2; Meloy 1988, pp. 35-37), meaning that the extremes scored similar in my correlations to Eysenck's pathological group. This makes good sense since the extremes in a normal group would be the hi/low of Eysenck's subject group.

The second reason for the breakdown of the P/TM trait in normal subject populations is best explained by a correlation study that Dr. Pierce Howard conducted on my data in 2006 (Howard & Howard 2006, pp. 62–63) (see *Table* 8.8). Howard found a strong correlation between the E (.65) and the N (.64) traits of EPQ-R and the Big Five E and N respectively, with some strong loadings in sub-traits as well (especially sub-traits in N, E, and A). When, however, Howard analyzed the P/TM trait with the Big Five, he found moderate negative "loadings" on the Big Five C (Consolidation) trait (-.32), and moderate loadings on the Big Five sub-traits N1: Worry (-.33), C1: Thoroughness (-.24), C2: Organization (-.39), and C5: Methodicalness (-.31). Howard argued that the EPQ-R's P/TM scale appeared "to measure something akin to chaos" (Howard & Howard 2006, p. 63).

Table 8.8   Howard & McCorkle Correlation Analysis of Big Five and Eysenck EPQ-R

N=57 (Big Five down and EPQ-R across)

N=57	N	E	P/TM	L
N	0.64	0.21	-0.02	-0.28
E	-0.14	0.65	-0.03	0.03
O	-0.14	0.19	0.15	-0.08
A	0.04	-0.24	-0.11	0.41
C	-0.14	0.01	-0.32	0.07
N.1	0.40	-0.02	-0.33	-0.11
N.2	0.38	0.29	0.14	-0.34
N.3	0.29	0.08	0.05	-0.18
N.4	0.48	0.14	0.09	-0.20
E.1	0.20	0.66	0.07	-0.15
E.2	0.12	0.37	0.03	0.20
E.3	-0.03	0.24	-0.08	0.24
E.4	-0.12	0.29	-0.06	-0.40
E.5	-0.05	0.07	-0.16	0.24
E.6	0.14	0.25	0.04	0.03
O.1	-0.10	0.27	0.14	-0.20
O.2	-0.05	-0.01	0.06	-0.02
O.3	-0.18	0.13	0.08	-0.08
O.4	-0.05	0.14	0.20	0.04
A.1	0.12	0.32	0.12	0.15
A.2	-0.12	-0.23	-0.27	0.51
A.3	0.11	0.15	0.04	0.31

Table 8.8 continued				
A.4	-0.01	-0.37	-0.24	0.29
A.5	0.01	-0.46	0.00	0.22
C.1	-0.12	-0.03	-0.24	0.12
C.2	0.02	0.05	-0.39	-0.14
C.3	-0.16	0.26	-0.11	-0.05
C.4	-0.31	-0.22	-0.04	0.08
C.5	0.22	-0.03	-0.31	0.22

This may provide evidence to support the claim that the typical responses to dead bodies by psychotics may be the result of a dysfunction in the cognitive systems involved when a person is confronted with a dead body stimulus. This observation, along with original groups that Eysenck used in his construction of the EPQ-R, might argue that P/TM is unable to measure normal populations, especially the subjects closer to the means. However, the Big Five, a later but well researched instrument, was designed to measure five traits (N, E, O, A, and C) on normal subject populations.

The normal population

If *some* of the observations toward the pathological group are correct Contagion-avoidance (seen in disgust), Person-file, and Predation systems are intimately related. It would also appear that systems such as Animacy, and Intuitive Psychology might be related. Therefore, I performed a simple correlation analysis on the five systems, as seen in *Table* 8.9.

Table 8.9 Correlation between Five Mental Systems Activated by Dead Bodies

N=57	Animacy	Predation	Intuitive Psychology	Peson-file	Contagion
Animacy System	1	0.07	0.92	0.55	0.71
Predation System	0.07	1	0.02	0.61	0.11
Intuitive Psychology	0.92	–0.02	1	0.49	0.56
Person-File System	0.55	0.61	0.49	1	0.36
Contagion System	0.71	0.11	0.56	0.36	1

Bold is significant at the 0.01 level

This simple correlation between Boyer's five systems illustrates several important factors concerning the five systems. Animacy, Intuitive Psychology, and Contagion (now Contagion-avoidance) are significantly related to one another. It would appear that the Animacy system and the Predation system (as identified in the theory of HADD) are not related systems. Therefore, I argue that HADD is the reflexive activation of not only movement awareness, but the potentiality of hostile predator awareness. If these two systems are not measuring the same thing, I argue that the Predation system measures movement for preservation without complex thinking about animacy, while the Animacy system measures highly complex mental processing about a theory of animacy, or as Leslie argues, a Theory of Body (ToBy) (Leslie 1994). This would explain the high correlation between the Animacy system and the Intuitive Psychology system. They both involve highly complex mental processing about purposeful movement and the possible intent of an agent.

Both the Animacy, Intuitive Psychology, and Contagion-avoidance systems and the Predation system (which are not related to each other) correlate to the Person-file system, suggesting that highly complex thinking about agents is involved in the activation and retrieval of important information concerning persons. Nevertheless, the stronger correlation between the Predation and Person-file systems suggests that less complex, possibly more instinctual information is exchanged between the two systems. So, person-file would appear to be a type of situational memory about agents i.e., moving bush + dark outside + past experience = *potential* predator.

If this is the case, and I think there is good reason to claim the connection, Person-file system should really be categorized as "Agent–file" system with a sub-category of Person–file, since predators are not all in fact other people. This would also make sense that HADD would utilize past experience collected on agents and situations and trigger a *precautionary* response.

In the next chapter, bolstered by the experimental studies that I have done, I will use Boyer & Liénard's model (2006b) to argue that: (1) Psychotics have a dysfunction in the cognitive systems responsible for reacting to dead bodies, (2) the normal functioning cognitive systems include the Hazard-Precaution System (Contagion/Contamination system), Person-file System, and these together (and maybe a half dozen other systems) tend to have the behavioral output of ritualized religious disposal, and (3) the variation in the normal population Psychoticism/Tough-mindedness scores (and subsequent variation in responses to dead bodies) are reflected in the variation in collective rituals disposing of dead bodies.

Summary

In Chapter Eight, I advanced the hypothesis that social intelligence, especially Theory of Mind, was involved in the by-product of ritualized behavior. Based upon my own fieldwork and archival research, I constructed a series of experiments involving vignettes to tease out participants' responses to scenarios involving dead bodies in various states. I argued that certain personality traits (most notably Psychoticism/Tough-mindedness and Neuroticism) were strong indicators in regard to how disgusted the participants would score. Using several well-tested inventories to compare and measure personality, disgust, and my own vignettes (The DIG 5), I concluded that disgust was inversely proportional to high scores in Psychoticism/Tough-mindedness and Extraversion. The higher the scores on these personality traits the lower the disgust by individuals concerning dead bodies in various states of decomposition. Moreover, disgust and contagion-avoidance toward dead bodies were found to be only slightly related in regard to each other.

Furthermore, I found a significant realtionship in the quantitative data between contagion-avoidance toward dead bodies in relation to *Animacy* (i.e., theory of movement) and *Theory of Mind* (i.e., the processing of an agent's—now dead—mental feelings, emotions, and intentions). I concluded that the quantitative data supported the theory that ritualized disposal of dead bodies was a by-product of social intelligence and the mis-firing of biological warning systems (BWS). Thus, I suggested that ritualized corpse disposal was not about biological threats, but about mentally processing dead agents and their mental states.

Also in this chapter, I proposed a hypothesis on why ritualized behavior, though widespread, was so variable from culture to culture. I argued that human beings were genetically, developmentally, and culturally primed to handle dead bodies in various ways, measurable by personality traits. These traits scored like a stereo equalizer, where some subjects were EQ-d for high/low disgust towards corpses, and others were EQ-d high/low for ritualized behavior towards dead bodies. Because humans were all individually different in their EQ (i.e., emotional quotient), putting them together in social groups would have produced a different result each and almost every time. In other words, individuality in humans is based on horizontal segmentation (e.g., Bell curve, continuum) in regard to reactions to corpse stimuli thus producing a varied response as groups performing these behaviors in rituals.

Chapter Nine

Memes, Genes, and Dead Machines

General Discussion

Introduction

In the light of all that I have argued up to this point and, in order to developing a deeper explanatory understanding of the processes involved in the ritualized disposal of dead bodies. I will propose a cognitive model of such behavior. This model will, I believe, demonstrate or at least suggest why a cognitive approach to the disposal of human bodies is important and necessary for any explanatory theories. Before doing so it may be helpful to reiterate some points made previously:

1. Theories that appeal primarily to notions of symbolism and meaning are not sufficient to explain the disposal of dead bodies (but they may be of value—see point five) especially when cognitive and evolutionary considerations are involved.

2. The widespread tendency to dispose of dead bodies is a behavioral output of an *aggregate* of evolved cognitive systems.

3. Any adaptive advantage the disposal of dead bodies provides is not because dead bodies are biologically dangerous and their removal protects humans from that danger.

4. The calibration of these systems begins in humans at a very early age and continues throughout young adulthood.

5. Hazard-Management systems (P. Boyer & Liénard 2006b) are implicated in the tendency to dispose of dead bodies in particular *(ritualized)* ways.

6. The *religious* ritualized disposal of dead bodies is the result of a highly complex mental process concerning social intelligence, symbolism, and meaning.

The Mental Culture of Dead Agents

A. High Psychoticism/Tough-mindedness scores

I. Low disgust

High P/TM subjects exhibit very low levels of disgust. Extremely unmoved by potential biohazards, these subjects appear to not be bothered by fresh corpses (wet) or skeletons (dry). This was apparent in Vignettes 3 (N=53, α = .801) where they garnered low disgust scores when asked questions about handling a fresh corpse, eating food in the near vicinity of a corpse (questions 3, 4, and 5), or even working with a cadaver that dies of an infectious disease (question 25). High P/TM subjects' answers to questions following Vignette 5 (N=53, α = .841) scored low on disgust in regard to skeletons (dry remains). Their answers indicated that they didn't mind touching them and were not concerned about any perceived contagion from infectious diseases that may have contributed to the death of these individuals (question 23, 25rev).

II. High tendency to ignore Person-file inferences

In questions following Vignettes no. 2 (N=53, α = .840) and no. 4 (N=53, α = .654), high P/TM subjects regularly scored low on questions that refer to the Person-file system. This was not just in response to scenarios that involved individuals with whom they were unfamiliar (strangers). Responses to questions about Vignette 6 (N=53, α = .678) indicate that High P/TM subjects did not appear to be bothered by corpses even if they knew the person.

B. Low Psychoticism/Tough-mindedness scores

I. High disgust

Low P/TM subjects garnered extremely high disgust scores on questions concerning corpse stimuli. On questions following Vignette no. 1 (N=53, α = .589), low P/TM subject responses indicated that they wanted someone else (a professional) to clean, touch, and dispose of the body (questions 25, 26) and they scored high with regard to burial of the corpse (13). In addition, low P/TM subject's answers to questions about Vignette no. 3 (N=53, α = .801) indicated that they would be bothered if they had to take an anatomy course and would prefer to not mix eating (even if it was someone else eating) with having to touch the corpse (questions 2, 3, 4, and 5). The Low P/TM subjects generally didn't want to work on a cadaver, especially if it had died of an infectious disease (question, 25). Answers to questions after Vignette no. 2 (N=53, α = .771) indicate that the low P/TM subjects did not want to buy a house if someone had been killed there, even if it had been professionally cleaned (questions, 17, 18, 25, and 27).

II.   Low tendency to ignore Person-file inferences

These same low P/TM subjects scored high in questions about Person-file issues even if they didn't know the corpse. The low P/TM subjects scored extremely high in vignette no. 2 (N=53, α = .840), on questions measuring Person-file activation, even if the subjects did not know the deceased. It was also evident from responses to questions about Vignette no. 3 (N=53, α =.729) that low P/TM subjects didn't want to work on a cadaver (even a person they didn't know). Vignette no. 4 (N=53, α = .654) describes the discovery of a corpse on the beach. The Low P/TM subjects were extremely disgusted by this but were unwilling to leave the body on the beach even to get help (question 11). Furthermore, they scored high (appeared to be extremely bothered), if the corpse was disposed of in an inappropriate way (question 19, 27) and they indicated that this dead person should be buried/cremated even if they were missing pieces of their body (questions 20, 21) or if they were a violent criminal (question 28).

C. Normal population (middle of continuum)

I.   Similar scores for both disgust and attention to Person-file inferences

Responses to questions about contagion-avoidance/disgust and the Person-file system by normal subjects indicated a similar degree of preoccupation with both. It is not that they are measuring the same thing, because they clearly are independent systems. However, there is a significant correlation (N=57, .36, significance of .01) between these two systems to suggest that there is a relationship between the two.

II. Unlike in extreme Psychoticism instances (and indication of the dysfunction of involved cognitive systems) systems responsible for BOTH disgust reactions and person-file inferences are triggered and result in the detection of *potential* threats.

Apparently, extreme P/TM subjects appear to have a "cognitive dissonance" among their cognitive systems. Disgust, Contagion-avoidance, and HADD appear to be almost turned off in the high P/TM subjects, and hypersensitive in the low P/TM subjects. High P/TM subjects appear highly sensitive to Animacy and ToMM. This can be seen most explicitly in Vignette no. 5, where high P/TM subjects were not bothered by skeletons, unless they activated ToMM (N=53, α = .70) and "appeared to be looking at them" (question, 8) or "twitched" (question 7).

III. HPS triggered – potential threats could span multiple domains

The data seems to offer evidence that the Hazard-Precaution model proposed by Boyer and Liénard (2006b) does not appear to be activated simply by the sense of smell. It appears that hazard management systems in general may in fact be activated across multiple domains, especially with regards to highly complex thinking about agents, their states, intention, and inferences about such things. This can be seen in the relationship between the Contagion-avoidance system and the Animacy and Intuitive Psychology systems (N=43, .71 and .56 respectively, significance to the .01 level). Possible *potential* threat domains are:

1. social threat

2. intrusive thoughts

3. contamination/contagion

D. Contamination/Contagion and Person-file

Contagion-avoidance measures may be the behavioral outputs of cognitive systems triggered by a potential threat, as opposed to an imminent threat (see Boyer and Liénard 2006a, 2006b). As Rozin has claimed, disgust is a "complex emotion" that is triggered by anxiety caused by an unconscious activation of certain systems, which "remind" us of our animal past (Miller 1997, p. 6). Apparently, the activation of this complex emotion (disgust and contagion) appears related to my claims concerning Mithen's thesis. Humans wish to escape their animal past, yet their cognitive architecture is formed by an evolved mental system from early humans. Therefore, our mental systems are activated for disgust and contagion-avoidance because we have an evolved social intelligence that is highly sensitive to information and inferences about other agents. In addition, dead bodies stimulate/activate these mental systems.

Hazard-Precaution systems (HPS) make sure that humans pay attention to these important inferences. Humans, and in this case dead humans (agents), are extremely salient representations that activate specialized mental systems, and the HPS is triggered to reinforce any potential behavioral output. We "handle" dead bodies, precisely because these are dead agents and our cognitive hardware has developed a special precision to process information and inferences about agents. A dead agent is therefore a by-product of this mental activation and processing. Nevertheless, it is a very old by-product which might have certain selective advantages.

I.   Contamination/Contagion resolution – disposal

It seems quite clear from the archival, ethnographic, and experimental data that corpses cause contagion-avoidance for reasons that have very little to do with smell. In fact throughout my vignettes, especially salient in Vignette no. 4 in Contagion-avoidance (N=53, α = .686), normal subjects were unwilling to leave the body, even to get the authorities (question 4rev), though many of them felt the corpse was disgusting and/or contagious. In the Person-file activation of Vignette no. 4 (N=53, .654), subjects simply were unwilling to leave the beach without someone staying with the corpse (question 11). In other words, the corpse might stimulate contagion-avoidance, but not over the activation that some kind of disposal must occur.

II.   Person-file resolution – retention/propriety

What we also can infer from the data is that, in the first instance, Person-file activation appears to be a cause for the suppression of the HPS by humans, as in the case of the above protection of the corpse until a disposal can take

place. In fact, it would appear that the HPS caused anxiety and is not allevi-
ated until a disposal can take place. So, Person-file reinforces the salience of
the HPS tags. The corpse, regardless of who the person is (obviously graded by
knowing the deceased) activates Person-file to elicit a disposal, even when disgust and contagion-avoidance are triggered. Similarly, the high correlation between the Person–file and Predation systems suggests that the HPS might be
turned down (or off) in the behavior of handling dead bodies. This, however,
causes Person–file systems to activate highly salient memories about the deceased, causing certain systems not to turn off theory of mind in responses to
dead bodies, or activating another type of system that represents the dead person as psychologically continuing, or as I have coined PARA for *Psychological
Agency Representation Activation*. Further experimental work might be done to
tease out whether the human Intuitive Psychology system doesn't turn off in
response to a corpse, or if something else (PARA) turns on.

E. Resulting Potential Threats

(Social offense, contamination) activates Hazard-Precaution System

It is now worth discussing in more detail, the Boyer and Liénard proposal of a
Hazard-Precaution model and its relationship to other systems activated by
dead agents. Earlier in *Religion Explained*, Boyer names two systems in particular that are activated as precautionary systems to real or potential dangers, the
Predation and Contagion systems (2001, pp. 223-24). These systems are not
only independent systems (as shown in *Figure 9.1*), but they may have distinct
specialized devices which help in their activation (i.e., HADD and Disgust, respectively).

These types of specialized systems, probably for good evolutionary reasons,
utilize specific mechanisms such as HADD and Disgust, because these systems
are probably hypersensitive for selective reasons. It is better for HADD or Disgust to be triggered in multiple false alarms, rather than to be eaten by a potential predator, or to consume poison berries etc. Therefore, for important
evolutionary reasons, humans developed systems that utilized these important
survival systems and mechanisms. Since, as Mithen's argument claims, human
minds developed from extremely specialized, task-oriented systems to a cognitively fluid generalized system; Predation systems and Contagion-avoidance

systems developed and utilized more specific mechanisms. In addition, the Hazard-Precaution system was then able to inform other systems of potential dangers, even if they transcend what the specialized systems were originally designed to handle (i.e., actual threats). Thus, the Hazard-Precaution system spans multiple domains because potential dangers are not limited to predators and poison berries.

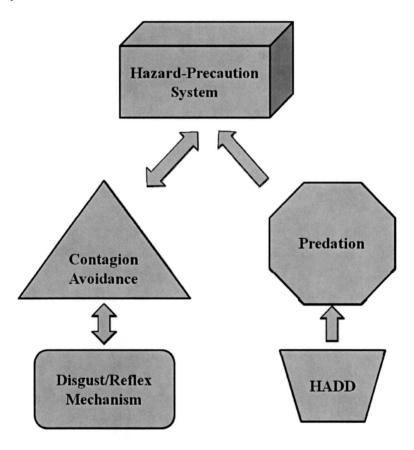

Figure 9.1 Diagram of Hazard-Precaution System

I.   Introduces potential threats

a. Intrusive thoughts – "It is wrong to dispose of my friend."

The Hazard-Precaution system (HPS) is most probably important in the development of ritualized disposal of bodies. They cause humans to feel anxiety in the presence of a corpse. So, simply throwing away a deceased person as a piece of garbage is usually not an option. Such notions as, "It is wrong to dispose of my friend or family member, or even a stranger" are generally felt by individuals. The stimulation of the HPS in addition to the activation of the Person-file system triggers a ritualized response by the majority of normal humans.

b.   Social status – Take action that will not damage status

The activation of HPS also informs other mental systems in regard to social intelligence. The modern mind has developed as a distinct cognitive architecture that processes multiple inferences about social data. The kinds of social behaviors and inferences that anthropologists have observed (including me) is reinforced by the activation of the HPS. Humans have developed as highly complex social creatures, where breaking certain types of social relationships, or inferences about social relationships, might be harmed without the activation of the HPS.

c.   Contamination

Anxiety

One of the more compelling aspects of human behavior (that is informed by mental systems) activated by a corpse, is the precipitation of anxiety which these activations cause. In both OCD patients and high P/TM psychotics, subjects are compelled to perform certain ritualized actions to alleviate the anxiety. Frequently the anxiety is never really eased; in fact, it may cause the subject to become more obsessed or to engage in the compulsion to perform highly ritualized activities. As Boyer & Liénard (2006a, 2006b) and Fiske and his colleagues suggest (Dulaney & Fiske 1994; Fiske & Haslam 1997), it would appear that collective rituals involve many of the same types of compulsions, especially as they pertain to ideas of contamination (i.e., washing, changing clothes, feeling contaminated) or avoidance of such contagion (i.e., fear, anxiety, or simply avoiding the body or anyone or anything that has come into contact with the body).

Anxiety appears to be a powerful motivating biological/psychological force that re-enforces certain mental systems to be activated to "process" how we should "handle" the problem by behavioral responses, in other words, performing a certain action to try to ease the anxiety that we feel. This may in fact elicit contamination type representations as a by-product of the activation of the Hazard-Precaution System (specifically Contagion-avoidance), which has been triggered by "potential" hazards associated with the activation of other mental systems involving dead bodies. Dead bodies are not especially dangerous; however, our minds have an extremely difficult time representing them in ways that don't activate contamination and avoidance. However, it is better in evolutionary terms to trigger such Hazard-Precaution systems, rather than to be wrong once. This may in fact be why Contagion-avoidance is so directly related to Animacy and Intuitive Psychology concerning dead bodies, it takes highly complex mental systems to shut off the Hazard-Precaution system (if at all) and to represent the "potential" danger as either "actual" danger or not dangerous at all.

d.   Corpse/Contagion resolution–disposal contradicts Person-file resolution–retention/propriety

What does appear to be the case, on the basis of the data, is that the simple disposal of humans is complicated by the mental activation of the Person-file system. As seen earlier in the vignettes, humans appear to feel the need to "protect" the corpse until it can receive a ritualized disposal. Even when the subjects appeared not to know the individual, they were still inclined to protect, salvage, keep together anatomical parts, and not just leave the corpse where it lay, even to the point of going to get help. Ordinary disposal, for example in the garbage disposal, is sufficiently outweighed by the activation of the Person-file that this dead body is not to be treated like other garbage or dead things. Apparently a corpse is something much more significant than just an object that has ceased to have any function (i.e., it is dead). In fact, as I have argued before, this may be directly due to the evolution of human social intelligence, where agency, states of agents, intentions and inferences are of crucial importance to our day to day lives. So, when the human Person-file system is activated in response to a dead body there are serious consequences (anxiety for one) that are produced if we do not dispose of it in certain ways.

e.   Doubts about closure

One of the more salient points of the activation of Person-file and Intuitive Psychology systems is the ongoing problem of processing a dead physical agent from their represented psychological state. I have coined this representation as the PARA (Psychological Agency Representation Activation), where humans appear to know a person is biologically and physically dead; however, they do not appear to be able process whether they are psychologically dead.[1] This motivates their behavior to treat dead bodies in unusual ways, as if they were living (as in cultural observations), or mentally to represent the dead person as still "ongoing" somewhere. Closure of this problem appears to be highly unstable; in fact, doctrinal representation systems appear to "control" the PARA with extensive and explicitly re-enforced doctrinal constraints. Nevertheless, the doctrinal representation systems do not appear to "control" the PARA sufficiently, because the natural default is an ongoing representation that needs repeated performances to alleviate closure concerns. Relics actually may expose the fragility of doctrinal control over the PARA. Relics are found in both doctrinal and non-doctrinal representation systems, as discussed earlier in the North American and Indian Buddhist doctrinal examples, as well as early human and Neanderthal, and the South Asian tsunami disposal behaviors.

Outputs consistent with behavioral predictions of the Hazard-Precaution system theory *and* disposal urges

Ritualized actions

Ritualized actions are performed because they activate multiple mental systems that are "tagged" by the HPS, which cause humans to perform rigid, repetitive, non haphazard, goal-demoted activity. These actions take various cultural forms. These same systems are employed in pathological behaviors (e.g., OCD,

---

[1] Recent experimental evidence by Richert and Harris (2006) suggests that young children may represent dead agents through different "folk taxonomies," rather than Cartesian dualism (i.e. mind and body). According to their findings, "children who have been exposed to the idea of a soul differentiate the soul from the mind and the brain. Furthermore, children see the specific function of the soul as being spiritual in nature rather than cognitive and biological" (p. 425). In addition, they write, "Perhaps...that the concept of a soul arises from the innate predisposition to treat people differently from objects" (p. 424).

Psychoticism), childhood behavior that identifies calibration of these systems, and collective ritualized activity (rituals).

Disposal

Disposal of dead bodies appears to be a behavior that humans have participated in for tens, if not hundreds of thousands of years, resulting in ritualized disposal towards dead bodies presented in material evidence between fifty to one hundred and fifty thousand years ago. Moreover, the better the material and historical record, the more it appears that these disposals were ritualized behaviors resulting in religious ritualized disposals in the last several thousand years. This increase may be due to the rise of professional guilds of disposal experts. So, disposal behavior employs an evolutionary and historical inquiry to account for the various types of disposal actions, humans have performed on dead bodies.

Nota bene

Imminent threat systems NOT triggered

The Hazard-Precaution system (HPS) that is activated appears to be much more complex than previously argued. In fact, one of the special qualities of the Hazard-Precaution model is that it identifies not only "real" threats as in "fight or flight" scenarios; it also detects much more complex "potential" threats to humans. By utilizing fluidity between specific devices (i.e., HADD, Disgust), the Hazard-Precaution system is able to be triggered by both kinds of threats, but it appears that HPS mainly is triggered in response to "potential" threats much more than "actual" threats. This is the case with dead bodies where the scientific data (e.g., CDC, WHO, and PAHO) clearly shows that dead bodies do not pose an actual, imminent threat. HPS is activated because a dead body violates multiple expectations about its ontological state (i.e., agents do not cease to be agents very easily once they are given this ontological status). Moreover, it appears that Hazard-Precaution models of ritualized behavior and religious ritualized behaviors are important to understand the complicated relationship between cognitive systems and behavioral output construed by them (i.e., rituals). It appears that cognitive fluidity makes the mental architecture of humans into a very *clever* creature that develops the recognition of potential threats as a selection advantage in human evolution.

Religious, ritualized disposal of dead bodies is a spandrel *or* by-product.

Religious ritualized disposals are effectively a by-product of the evolved cognitive architecture of the human mind. By extension, dead bodies activate counterintuitive representations of ontological violations in human minds, causing many of the ritualized disposals (if not all) to be what we might categorize as "religious" types of actions. All dead bodies stimulate these counterintuitive (religious) representations in normal human minds (in various ways). In addition, religious experts in disposal have taken these representations and collected them into texts and collective practices, passing them down through history. This is not to say that religious ritualized disposal of dead bodies does not present a selective advantage to humans, there may be other possible explanatory claims for selective advantages concerning the ritualized disposal of dead bodies.[2] Nevertheless, it does not appear possible (at this point in evolutionary time) to be able distinguish between selective advantage in conspecific fitness and cultural "noise" that is observed in collective ritualized disposals in regard to dead human bodies (see *Figure* 9.2).

---

[2] I have suggested elsewhere (McCorkle 2008a; *forthcoming* –*b*) that although ritualized disposal is a naturally occurring by-product of complex mental processes, humans appear to have used these representations in ways that may have benefitted social groups by generating niches of culture. Thus, this by-product becomes a spandrel for complex cultural construction that aids in the generation of meaning in horizontal space, yet the material remains of corpses, relics, and religious ritualized locations aid in the stability of the vertical transmission of culture.

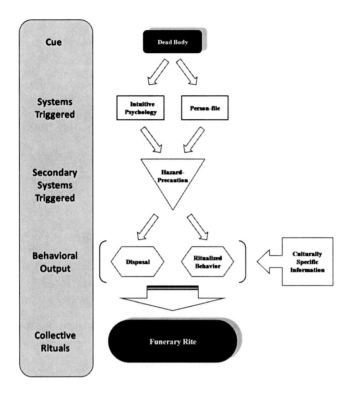

Figure 9.2 Diagram of Ritualized Disposal

A Cognitive Ethnography for Mortuary Behavior

I have been rather critical of anthropological theories (though I claim they are still important and have provided extremely precise observational details of the physical disposal of corpses and behavior surrounding them). In fact, I claim that the combination of the methods and theories postulated in the disciplines of anthropology and psychology, as seen in the *cognitive science of religion* are necessary to explain these cultural behaviors.[3] Here I list a few observations

[3] I, like Strauss and Quinn (1997) and Whitehouse (2004, 2007), argue for the building of a mature corpus of scientific knowledge, based upon ethnographic theory and fieldwork. Both *evolutionary psychology* and the *cognitive science of religion* premise their disciplines by refined, descriptive methodologies found in anthropological and other social/behavioral sciences. The rejection of older theories, theorists, and methodologies would simply be akin to throwing the proverbial "baby out with the bathwater." Here Whitehouse writes, "the study of religion *can*

(some exact and some paraphrased) by Émile Durkheim from *The Elementary Forms of Religious Life* (1976, pp. 434-61) about some beliefs surrounding the circumstance of someone's death:

1. Everything that is connected to the dead man is contagious.

2. This contagion causes the body to be handled in a *religious* not profane way.

3. These rites usually commence as soon as the death occurs.

4. The death of an individual usually requires a certain etiquette, which involves an explicit form of grief.

5. The most severe are those that are related (kinship) to the dead man.

6. Women are required to perform certain severe obligations surrounding death.

7. The actions surrounding these rituals are performed again and again.

8. The signs of grief are mixed with anger in these mourning rituals.

9. The anger may result in an action of attack, though it is usually symbolic.

10. The attack may involve a relic from the corpse.

11. The death demands the shedding of blood, either symbolically or in reality.

12. The living person may be good; however, once dead he becomes malevolent.

13. These groups must find a victim (real or imagined) to discharge their collective pain upon.

14. Mourning rituals deal with the problems caused by the death. The very things that make them arise also help them neutralize.

15. Since the essence of the dead person needs to receive the forms of sacrifice, grief etc. there must be a trace separate from the body that doesn't decompose. This is why the notion of the soul arises.

---

leave a legacy for the future, it *can* generate truly *cumulative* forms of knowledge, but this requires a different kind of approach to theory building. We need approaches that are willing to salvage old materials...based on a wide cooperation...rather than on the kind of competitive aesthetics popular in many humanities disciplines today, which so often privileges critical originality over theoretical precision and empirical productivity" (2004, pp. 172-73) (italics in original).

All of the above observations are of the kinds of beliefs that surround the ritualized behavior that humans engage in when a person dies. All of these observations by Durkheim can be explained at the cognitive level, which Durkheim and his followers claimed was not possible outside of "social" observations.[4] This clearly is not case, based upon the account I have offered in this monograph.

As seen in the Appendix, questions following Vignette No. 4 (with significant correlations) asked:

4.8   The intestines of the drowning victim are visibly hanging outside of the body. You put them back into the person's body?

4.9   You see the person's arm floating out in the water. You swim out and grab it?

4.11   You think it is wrong to leave the body on the beach without some one staying with it?

4.18   This experience would cause you a great deal of anxiety?

4.19   You would tell the authorities to stop, if they were disrespectful in handling the body?

4.20   You think the person would want to be buried/cremated even if they were missing most of their body to a shark attack?

4.21   You think that this person would want to be buried/cremated even if they were missing their head?

---

[4] This important methodological point has been taken up by Sperber (1985) and Lawson & McCauley (1990). Implicit (if not explicit) in this Durkheimian stance is the argument that ethnographic fieldwork reveals "social" and material facts (see also Malinowski 2008/1922). Moreover, this promotes the theory that only external actions are material, similar to problems seen in arguments concerning Cartesian dualism, where the body is material, but many times the mind (or mental processes) is considered non-material. Later, anthropologists such as E.E. Evans-Pritchard (1937, 1956) and Clifford Geertz (1973) argued that ethnographic data would reveal theory in each specific context, and that universal theories to explain culture were a thing of the past. In fact, Evans-Pritchard fieldwork, considered by many in anthropology as the example *par excellence* of descriptive ethnography, offers almost no evidence of a universal theory, especially in regard to religion (Pals 2006, pp. 229-59). However, as Lawson and McCauley write, "Sperber (1985) argues, theoretical advances in anthropology await neither more nor more complete ethnographies (though, theoretical progress may subsequently require *new sorts* of ethnographies). All data-gathering is theoretically inspired....Theories guide interpretation. No datum is self interpreting" (Lawson & McCauley 1990, p. 10) (italics in original).

4.25   You are willing to help the victim knowing that they died from an infectious disease?

4.26   You are willing to help the victim even though the locals say that she/he is cursed?

4.27   You feel the ghost/spirit of the person is watching how you handle the body?

4.28   You would help this person even if you knew that they were a violent criminal (child molester, murderer, terrorist)?

4.4rev   You [don't] leave the body where it is and go tell the authorities?

It seems clear from the relationships (and strong correlations) between the questions that preservation and protection of the freshly dead corpse is extremely important. Notice that principles such as contagion by biological threats, the relationship to the departed and possibly counterintuitive threats (curses) are not enough to cause the individual to cease in the protection and preservation of the dead body.

Whether it involves disposing of the corpse by means of encapsulation into a burial casket, sealing it in a vault, and covering it with earth six feet under the ground, or throwing it onto a large bonfire of wood, coal, or turf and setting the body on fire (cremation), the physical, biological body is in one way or another removed from the public sphere. If any of the actions necessary to accomplish this are not performed correctly, it is often the case that people will think that they are suffering from intentional misfortune at the hands of the dead person. In other words, a dead person is dangerous unless it has been disposed of in the proper way.

This feature is noted in Durkheim's observation No. 12, where the dead person is represented as malevolent after the death, even if they were considered by their peers as a good, nice, respectable person in life. Notice that in doctrinal (oral or written) traditions, which have a professional guild of religious experts such as dynastic Egypt, the physical remains are mummified and—along with wives, slaves, and pets—entombed in a sarcophagus, in a special room, and in a special building. These remains and locations are sealed along with harsh penalties for anyone who disturbs this entombment, via ancient laws and *counterintuitive* prohibitions (curses). These penalties might be easily manifested in many ways including the old king threatening the rule of the new regime by means of hauntings, ghostly appearances, or rising from the dead and replacing the new sovereign. Also, note Durkheim's number 15 where his notion of the soul directly corresponds to my claim of the Psychological Agency Representation Activation (PARA) caused by counterintuitive inferences with regard to theory of mind.

Once the physical remains have been disposed of sufficiently, the representation of the dead person sometimes enjoys a transmission advantage since the ritualized actions used to dispose of the dead body may be repeated by using the relics of the dead person. For example, if something happens to the community that revokes or questions the accuracy of the first ritualized action (i.e., it wasn't performed correctly the first time), then something malevolent happens to the community which they connect to an incorrect performance.

From Ritualized Compulsions to Ritual Scripts

Individual ritualized behavior occurs across most if not all domains: childhood behaviors, clinically diagnosed dysfunctions, salient life stages, and much of normal behavior (Boyer & Liénard 2006b). Some are examples of the system being calibrated in the case of a developing child or the dysfunctional cognitive systems involved in pathological cases. In other cases, they are what appear to be what we commonsensically would call ordinary, habitual action. For example, for ten years I put my pants on everyday starting with the left foot first. Then one day I *accidentally* put the right foot in first. Realizing my "mistake" I took them off and started over by putting the left leg in first. They are not collective rituals, but the same cognitive systems are responsible (to some extent) for the behavioral outputs exhibited.

Collective rituals are social activities, which is why, I argue, that they are so open to symbolism and meaning. This is because the types of mental systems that are part of an evolved cognitive social intelligence constrain them in this way. This also may be where some of the anthropological theoretical tradition may provide some insight. Collective rituals often include appeals to other agents. For example, there may be an individual performing some action but another (counterintuitive) agent is indirectly present in the action structure (Lawson & McCauley 1990; McCauley & Lawson 2002). In addition, as Whitehouse argues, when activities like *pūjā* are performed they, in fact, elicit a "limitless range of meanings" that might be attached to these representations, since they do not have explicit doctrinal constraints imposed upon them (2004, p. 96).

Why are relics so common in religious rituals?

A considerable amount of time has been spent in this monograph on the role, function, and transmission of rituals that contain relics, which are the former remains/cremains of dead bodies. Why are such relics so common in religious ritualized disposal of dead bodies? They appear in Whitehouse's (2004) "doctrinal" and "imagistic" *modes of religiosity* (discussed earlier), and they are included in both McCauley and Lawson's "special agent and patient/instrument" rituals (2002), meaning that they are used in non-repeated and repeated rituals.[5] For one, as I have already claimed, human remains (bones) are significantly hard to destroy on purpose either by cremation, by predators, or by natural elements. They are also a by-product of human existence, easily found throughout the world (which also may explain why these remains may naturally drive humans to generate symbolic meaning in regard to them [see Hertz 1960; Douglas 2003]). At almost every stage of human evolution, people seem to feel compelled to do *something* with dead bodies and the remains.

The relic is represented mentally in a very salient way. The physical relic provides the connection to a relevant mental representation, which is very open to the processes of symbolism and therefore to almost endless meaning.

---

[5] In fact as Whitehouse (Whitehouse & Martin 2004) has persuasively argued, the "doctrinal mode" was the result of domesticated agriculture and the rise of complex societies, not the product of writing and literacy (pp. 215-32). Moreover, the "doctrinal mode" may have actually "kick-started" literacy, not the opposite, by triggering the "emergence of routinized orthodoxies," or professional guilds of cultural experts (p. 228). Material evidence supports Whitehouse's hypothesis at archaeological sites such as, Choga Mish and Susa (in prehistoric southwestern Iran), and Ohalo, Levant, Mesopotamia, and Çatalhöyük (western Asia), where the doctrinal mode appears before the advent of complex writing systems (see Johnson 2004; Mithen 2004). In agreement with Whitehouse, I have argued elsewhere (McCorkle *forthcoming* –b) that the remains of dead bodies (especially relics) may have been salient tools to connect "imagistic" ritual behavior and full blown "doctrinal" ritual scripts diachronically and synchronically (i.e., the *Shang* oracle bones in pre-historic China, where early writing appears on the skeletal remains of animals and reptiles). See also Diamond (1995) for the cultural effects of domesticated agriculture.

This openness is the result of the activation of hospitable cognitive social intelligence systems and results in collective representations being easily spread throughout time and across space.

Relics and their mental representations are by their very nature extremely transmittable (physically hard to destroy and mentally hard to ignore). They also trigger many of the same systems a freshly dead corpse activates; therefore, mimicking the cues necessary to trigger religiously ritualized disposal of dead bodies initiating those activities to be performed again and again.

Conclusions

In the first chapter, I argued that humans have engaged in disposal behavior at least as far back as we have material evidence. Also, I claimed as the evidence became clearer through historical time, more and more archeological and historical data supported ritualized disposal of dead bodies. Furthermore, I argued that by the time of the appearance of large populations of humans, the historical data supported *religious* ritualized behaviors in regard to dead bodies. This specialized behavior appears to be directly related to the rise of cultural experts in religious ritual behavior, although it is not beyond the possibility that this behavior existed on small scales before these professional guilds.

In chapters two through five, I presented the problem of ritualized disposals in Buddhism in response to scholars who claimed "original, pristine, and monastic" Buddhists do not engage in these kinds of activities. In addition, I argued, that a "fictional" Buddhist religion presented in certain texts was proof of such behaviors (non-disposal), when in fact the evidence implies that Buddhists in early India (and South Asia) as well as Buddhists in other cultures and time periods have performed with great frequency religious ritualized disposals of dead bodies. This important fact is not limited to the laity; in fact, a great deal of evidence illustrates that monastic Buddhists were engaged in these kinds of special actions from the very origins of the Buddhist religion.

In Chapter Six, I argued that previous explanations of religious ritualized behavior failed, since they were unable to explain ritual behavior sufficiently because they were interpretation-based theories rooted in symbolism and meaning. These same cultural theories (some with great potential) were not sufficient (nor necessary) to explain why humans performed elaborate rituals towards dead bodies. However, their extensive database provided for a naturalistic (cognitive) and explanatory theory to be introduced.

In Chapter Seven, I provided an account of a cognitive theory of the ritualized disposal of dead bodies that relied on the adaptability of humans to get rid of potential dangers (like corpses). However, the forensic data offered evidence that disputed this cognitive model. An investigation of relevant scientific literature expanded and developed a new model for ritualized disposal.

In Chapter Eight, I reported the results of experiments that I designed to test the potentially salient features of mental systems activated by corpse stimuli and subjects that were differentiated by traits defined in personality theory. By using pathological models and normal populations, I formulated a new model of the ritualized disposal of dead bodies. In addition, this new model introduced material from a variety of recent scientific work on more general (but still highly reliable) cognitive models of ritualized behaviors. This new evidence, coupled with the experimental data and analysis conducted in this work, exposed salient features of the cognitive architecture of the human mind.

Finally in Chapter Nine, I described in detail several systems that are activated in response to dead bodies and why humans have evolved the particular behaviors informed by their activation. In doing so, I claimed to provide more insight into a cognitive model that might inform, if not explain, religious ritualized disposals of dead bodies as a pan-human phenomenon.

Appendix

Questions and Systems

System 1 – Animacy system (N=53)

(Correlations) α = .531

1.7	Terrie talks to John wherever he is now
1.8	Terrie thinks the hospital killed John
1.22	Terrie wants to embrace John one more time before he is buried/cremated
1.23	Terrie wants her ashes to be placed in the same burial urn as John's after she dies
1.29	Terrie feels that hospitals are places where people die

α = .873

2.3	One of the owners recently died
2.5	One of the owners died in the house
2.10	Someone was killed in the house in the nineteen-sixties
2.15	A bunch of people were killed in the house twenty years ago
2.19	The house is said to be haunted
2.25	Multiple people were killed in the house, but the house can be professionally cleaned
2.27	There were some fatalities in the house, but the house has been thoroughly cleaned by professionals
2.28	The reports of ghosts in the house are said to infect people with diseases
2.37	The house smells like ghosts
2.39	The house is haunted, but Fran and Taylor don't believe in ghosts

$\alpha = .810$

3.7   Your favorite part to work on is the eyes of the cadaver

3.12   The body twitches while you are cutting on it, you keep cutting anyway

3.13   The eyelid opens to reveal the eyes while you are touching the body. You close it again

3.14   (If the body has not been embalmed yet) you want to be the student who embalms the body with formaldehyde because you have heard this might make the body sit up on the table

3.24   You are willing to work on the body by yourself late at night

3.26   You are willing to work on a cadaver that is said to be cursed

$\alpha = .562$

4.9   You see the person's arm floating out in the water. You swim out and grab it

4.11   You think it is wrong to leave the body on the beach without someone staying with it

4.18   This experience would cause you a great deal of anxiety

4.19   You would tell the authorities to stop if they were disrespectful in handling the body

4.26   You are willing to help the victim even though the locals say that she/he is cursed

4.27   You feel the ghost/spirit of the person is watching how you handle the body

4.28   You would help this person even if you knew that they were a violent criminal (child molester, murderer, terrorist)

$\alpha = .874$

5.5   You notice several skeletons lying in burial chambers along the wall, so you investigate them

5.6   You don't mind touching these ancient remains

5.7   You touch the skeleton, even if it twitches

5.8   You don't mind looking at the skeleton even though it still appears to look at you

5.9   You would pick up one of the skeleton's arms that has fallen to the ground and put it back with the skeleton it belongs to

5.17rev You realize that this cave/tomb is cursed, so you [don't] want to leave

5.18rev This experience would [not] cause you a great deal of anxiety

5.28rev Soon after learning that the cave contained skeletal remains, you would [not] feel scared if you heard strange noises in the cave/tomb

α =.649

6.3   You think they are able to see what you do

6.4   You think they talk to you in your dreams from time to time

6.12   You think that they have ways of contacting you

6.27   You avoid the place where you had this experience to this day

6.28   If you hear a strange sound in close proximity to where this experience occured, you would leave that place as soon as possible

System 2 Predation/HADD system (N=53)

α =.651

1.4   Terrie thinks John is watching down on her in heaven

1.7   Terrie talks to John wherever he is now

1.8   Terrie thinks the hospital killed John

1.9   Terrie heard the doctors whispering before John died; she thinks they are hiding something from her about John

1.13   Terrie wants John to be buried in the ground

1.15   Terrie wants to be with John when he is moved from the hospital

1.22   Terrie wants to embrace John one more time before he is buried/cremated

α =.619

2.43   There are large butcher knives all over the house

2.44   The house used to be a clinic for the mentally ill

α = .599

3. 1   You feel anxious about starting the class

3.19   You would tell your classmates to stop if they were disrespectful in handling the body

3.20   You think the person would want to be buried/cremated after the class/research is concluded

3.21   You think that even though most of the organs (brain, heart, kidneys, lungs, liver etc.) have been used in donations to other patients, this cadaver should still be buried/cremated

3.30   You think that others might find taking a questionnaire like this uncomfortable to them

3.7rev Your favorite part to work on is [isn't] the eyes of the cadaver

α = .620

4.19   You would tell the authorities to stop if they were disrespectful in handling the body

4.20   You think the person would want to be buried/cremated even if they were missing most of their body to a shark attack

4.21   You think that this person would want to be buried/cremated even if they were missing their head

4.27   You feel the ghost/spirit of the person is watching how you handle the body

4.28   You would help this person even if you knew that they were a violent criminal (child molester, murderer, terrorist)

4.30   You think that others might find taking a questionnaire like this uncomfortable to them

α = .638

5.12   You think that the skeleton's spirit is watching what you do in the cave/tomb

5.20   You think the person would want to be re-buried/cremated, even though it has been several hundred years since they died

5.24   You think this person would have wanted to be remembered in a special way

5.30   You think that others might find taking a questionnaire like this uncomfortable to them

5.8rev You don't [do] mind looking at the skeleton even though it still appears to look at you

α = .721

6.2   You think that person knows you saw them die
6.3   You think they are able to see what you do
6.9   You think they can see and hear what you do from time to time
6.12   You think that they have ways of contacting you
6.18   You saw them look at you for the last time and knew that they were ready to die
6.22   You think that if they had been buried/cremated incorrectly, they might be unhappy
6.30   You think that others might find taking a questionnaire like this uncomfortable to them

System 3 – Intuitive Psychology system (N=53)

α =.603

1.8   Terrie thinks the hospital killed John
1.9   Terrie heard the doctors whispering before John died she thinks they are hiding something from her about John
1.13   Terrie wants John to be buried in the ground
1.20   Terrie wants to hold John's hand one last time before burial/cremation
1.22   Terrie wants to embrace John one more time before he is buried/cremated

α = .775

2.3   One of the owners recently died
2.4   One of the owners' pets died in the house
2.7   One of the owners died in the house recently
2.16   There was a murder in the master bedroom
2.28   The reports of ghosts in the house are said to infect people with diseases
2.37   The house smells like ghosts

2.39   The house is haunted, but Fran and Taylor don't believe in ghosts

α = .770

3.7   Your favorite part to work on is the eyes of the cadaver

3.12   The body twitches while you are cutting on it, you keep cutting anyway

3.13   The eyelid opens to reveal the eyes while you are touching the body. You close it again

3.14   (If the body has not been embalmed yet) You want to be the student who embalms the body with formaldehyde because you have heard this might make the body sit up on the table

3.26   You are willing to work on a cadaver that is said to be cursed

α = .540

4.11   You think it is wrong to leave the body on the beach without someone staying with it

4.21   You think that this person would want to be buried/cremated even if they were missing their head

4.4rev   You [don't] leave the body where it is and go tell the authorities

α = .700

5.5   You notice several skeletons lying in burial chambers along the wall, so you investigate them

5.7   You touch the skeleton, even if it twitches

5.8   You don't mind looking at the skeleton even though it still appears to look at you

5.9   You would pick up one of the skeleton's arms that has fallen to the ground and put it back with the skeleton it belongs to

5.27   You feel the ghost/spirit of the person is watching how you handle the skeleton

5.28rev Soon after learning that the cave contained skeletal remains, you would feel scared if you heard strange noises in the cave/tomb

α =.636

6.27   You avoid the place where you had this experience to this day

6.28   If you hear a strange sound in close proximity to where this experi-
         ence occured, you would leave that place as soon as possible

System 4 – Person-file system (N=53)

α =.694

1.3   Terrie must have an explanation on why John died
1.4   Terrie thinks John is watching down on her in heaven
1.6   Terrie insists on cleaning John's body personally before they take him
         away
1.7   Terrie talks to John wherever he is now
1.8   Terrie thinks the hospital killed John
1.9   Terrie heard the doctors whispering before John died; she thinks they
         are hiding something from her about John
1.10   Terrie had a dream the night before that John was going to die. She
         thinks she may have caused his death
1.11   Terrie is afraid she may have contracted whatever made John ill
1.13   Terrie wants John to be buried in the ground
1.14   Terrie wants John to be buried in the ground without a coffin
1.15   Terrie wants to be with John when he is moved from the hospital
1.20   Terrie wants to hold John's hand one last time before bur-
         ial/cremation
1.21   Terrie wants to hang up John's clothes when she arrives back home
1.22   Terrie wants to embrace John one more time before he is bur-
         ied/cremated
1.23   Terrie wants her ashes to be placed in the same burial urn as John's
         after she dies
1.24   Terrie would like to take John's pillow from the hospital bed back
         home
1.29   Terrie feels that hospitals are places where people die

α = .840

2.2   The owners were separated recently
2.3   One of the owners recently died
2.4   One of the owners' pets died in the house

2.5	One of the owners died in the house
2.7	One of the owners died in the house recently
2.8	One of the owners died in the house a long time ago
2.12	Fran and Taylor knew the people who died in the house
2.13	Fran and Taylor were related to the person in the house who died
2.14	Fran and Taylor's childhood friend died in the house recently
2.42	All the owners of the house have died of a heart attack
2.44	The house used to be a clinic for the mentally ill

α = .729

3.7	Your favorite part to work on is the eyes of the cadaver
3.8	Your favorite part to work on is the heart of the cadaver
3.10	The recently deceased person died of cancer. You want to dissect the tumor

α = .654

4.11	You think it is wrong to leave the body on the beach without someone staying with it
4.19	You would tell the authorities to stop if they were disrespectful in handling the body
4.20	You think the person would want to be buried/cremated even if they were missing most of their body to a shark attack
4.21	You think that this person would want to be buried/cremated even if they were missing their head
4.27	You feel the ghost/spirit of the person is watching how you handle the body
4.28	You would help this person even if you knew that they were a violent criminal (child molester, murderer, terrorist)
4.30	You think that others might find taking a questionnaire like this uncomfortable to them

α = .567

5.12	You think that the skeleton's spirit is watching what you do in the cave/tomb

5.24   You think this person would have wanted to be remembered in a special way

α = .678
6.7   You talk about them from time to time
6.8   You tell people about this experience frequently
6.9   You think they can see and hear what you do from time to time
6.10   You wouldn't mind seeing them again, even if it was just their dead body
6.11   You think it is wrong for people to talk about them in an inappropriate manner
6.16   You remember what the smell was when you had this experience
6.17   You don't want to die like they did
6.23   You think holding them or being close to them at death might have made them more comfortable in dying
6.29   It makes you very sad to think of this experience

System 5 – Contagion-avoidance system (N=53)

α = .589
1.13   Terrie wants John to be buried in the ground
1.25   Terry would like someone else to handle John's body for her
1.26   Terrie wants a professional to clean and dispose of John's body

α = .771
2.17   Someone died in the kitchen
2.18   Someone died in the bathroom last week
2.25   Multiple people were killed in the house, but the house can be professionally cleaned
2.27   There were some fatalities in the house, but the house has been thoroughly cleaned by professionals
2.28   The reports of ghosts in the house are said to infect people with diseases
2.29   All the people who have died in the house have died of natural causes

2.37　The house smells like ghosts

2.38　The house smells like the ocean is near-by

2.40　The owner of the house died of AIDS, even though he was not at home at his/her death

2.44　The house used to be a clinic for the mentally ill

2.45　The house is said to breathe noxious fumes

2.46　The house is contagious to those who live in it

2.47　The house is disgusting to those who live in it

2.49　The house smells funny

$\alpha = .801$

3.2　You don't mind working with cadavers

3.3　The class is smack in the middle of lunchtime, so you bring your lunch

3.4　You don't mind if your professor eats her lunch in class while you work with the body

3.5　You eat your lunch periodically while you dissect the cadaver

3.9　Your favorite part to work on is the sexual organs of the cadaver

3.10　The recently deceased person died of cancer. You want to dissect the tumor

3.11　You enjoy draining the body of all its fluids and putting them into jars

3.13　The eyelid opens to reveal the eyes while you are touching the body. You close it again

3.14　(If the body has not been embalmed yet) You want to be the student who embalms the body with formaldehyde because you have heard this might make the body sit up on the table

3.16　You find it strange that the body is in bad shape, but doesn't have an odor

3.25　You are willing to work on a cadaver that died from an infectious disease

3.26　You are willing to work on a cadaver that is said to be cursed

3.28　You don't mind working on the body if you have a cold/flu/infection

α = .686

4.7   You eat your lunch after the ambulance takes the drowning victim away

4.8   The intestines of the drowning victim are visibly hanging outside of the body. You put them back into the person's body

4.9   You see the person's arm floating out in the water. You swim out and grab it.

4.22   You don't mind handling the body if it appears and smells normal

4.25   You are willing to help the victim knowing that they died from an infectious disease

4.26   You are willing to help the victim even though the locals say that she/he is cursed

4.4rev You [don't] leave the body where it is and go tell the authorities

α = .841

5.11   You think it is wrong to investigate an ancient burial tomb

5.13   After handling the bones you have an overwhelming urge to take a shower and wash your hands

5.14   You want to wash your clothes as soon as possible after handling the skeleton

5.15   You throw away your clothes as soon as possible after handling the skeleton

5.16   You find it strange that the skeleton is in great shape but has a terrible odor

5.17   You realize that this cave/tomb is cursed, so you want to leave

5.18   This experience would cause you a great deal of anxiety

5.23   You think skeletons are disgusting, but not infectious

5.6rev You don't [do] mind touching these ancient remains

5.25rev You are [not] willing to touch the skeleton, in spite of knowing that they died from an infectious disease

α = .657

6.14   You would wear their clothes, if they left them to you

6.23   You think holding them or being close to them at death might have made them more comfortable in dying

6.24   You would hold their hand or remain close even if they died from an infectious disease

6.25   You would be willing to help the funeral director move them from one location to another for burial/cremation

6.27rev You [don't] avoid the place where you had this experience to this day

Bibliography

Akira, H. (1990). *A History of Indian Buddhism: From Sakyamuni to early Mahayana* (P. Groner, Trans.). Honolulu: University of Hawaii Press.

Anderson, C. S. (1999). *Pain and its ending: The Four Noble Truths in the Theravada Buddhist canon.* Delhi: Motilal Banarsidass.

Axel, R. (2006). The molecular logic of smell. *Scientific American, 16,* 69–75.

Bachelor, S. (1997). *Buddhism without beliefs: A contemporary guide to awakening.* New York: Riverhead Books.

Bailey, G., & Mabbett, I. (2003). *The sociology of early Buddhism.* Cambridge: Cambridge University Press.

Baron-Cohen, S. (1997). *Mindblindness: An essay on autism and theory of mind.* Cambridge, MA & London: The MIT Press.

Barrett, J. L. (1999). Theological incorrectness: Cognitive constraint and the study of religion. *Method and Theory in the Study of Religion, 11,* 325–39.

—— (2000). Exploring the natural foundations of religion. *Trends in Cognitive Sciences, 4,* 29–34.

—— (2004). *Why would anyone believe in god?* Lanham, MD: AltaMira Press.

Bass, W. & Jefferson, J. (2003). *Death's acre: Inside the legendary forensic lab the Body Farm where the dead do tell tales.* New York: The Berkley Publishing Group.

Beal, S. (2004). *Buddhist records of the Western world.* London: Munshiram Manoharlal Publishers.

Belliveau, J., Rosen, B., Kantor, H., Rzedzian, R., Kennedy, D., McKinstry, R., Vevea, J., Cohen, M., Pykett, I., & Brady, T. (1990). Functional cerebral imaging by susceptibility-contrast nmr. *Magn Reson Med, 14,* 538–46.

Belliveau, J. K., D., McKinstry, R., Buchbinder, B., Weisscoff, R., Cohen, M., Vevea, J., Brady, T., & Rosen., B. (1991). Functional mapping of the human visual cortex by magnetic resonance imaging. *Science, 254,* 716–19.

Bering, J. (2002). Intuitive conceptions of dead agents' minds: The natural foundations of afterlife beliefs as phenomenological boundary. *Journal of Cognition and Culture, 2*(4), 263–308.

Bloch, M. (1974). Symbols, song, dance, and features of articluation: Is religion an extreme form of traditional authority. *European Journal of Sociology, 15,* 55–81.

—— (1982). Death, women, and power. In M. Bloch & J. Parry (Eds.), *Death and the regeneration of life* (pp. 211–230). Cambridge: Cambridge University Press.

—— (1991). *Prey into hunter: The politics of religious experience.* Cambridge: Cambridge University Press.

Bloch, M., & Parry, J. P. (1982). *Death and the regeneration of life.* Cambridge [Cambridgeshire]; New York: Cambridge University Press.

Boyer, P. (2001). *Religion explained: The evolutionary origins of religious thought.* New York: Basic Books.

Boyer, P., & Liénard, P. (2006a). Whence collective ritual? A cultural selection model of ritualized behavior. *American Anthropologist, 108*(4), 814-27.

—— (2006b). Why ritualized behavior? Precaution systems and action parsing in developmental, pathological, and cultural rituals. *Behavioral and Brain Sciences, 29,* 595-650.

Brekke, T. (2002). *Religious motivation and the origins of Buddhism: A social-psychological exploration on the origins of a world religion.* London: Routledge/Curzon.

Buckner, A. (1997). Ritual. In T. Barfield (Ed). *The dictionary of anthropology* (pp. 410-12). Oxford: Blackwell Publisher Ltd.

Buddhaghoṣa, B. (1964). *The path of purification (Visuddhimagga).* (B. Nyanomoli, Trans.). Colombo: A Semage.

Burkert, W. (1983). *Homo necans: The anthropology of ancient Greek sacrificial ritual and myth.* (P. Bing, Trans.). Berkeley and Los Angeles: University of California Press.

Buswell Jr., R. E. (1992). *The Zen monastic experience: Buddhist practice in contemporary Korea.* Princeton, NJ: Princeton University Press.

Clark, J. D., Beyene, Y., WoldeGabriel, G., Hart, W. K., Renne, P. R., Gilbert, H., Defleur, A., Suwa, G., Katoh, S., Ludwig, K. R., Boisserie, J. R., Asfaw, B., & White, T.D. (2003). Stratigraphic, chronological and behavioral contexts of Pleistocene Homo sapiens from Middle Awash, Ethiopia. *Nature, 423,* 452-71.

CNN. (2005). "Corpse plant" draws big crowds. Retrieved Monday November 21, from http://edition.cnn.com/2005/TECH/science/11/21/stinky.plant.ap/index.html

Collins, S. (1990). On the very idea of the Pali canon. *Journal of the Pali Text Society, 15,* 89-126.

Conze, E. (1958). *Triptika, Sutrapitika, Prajnaparamita, Vajracchedika.* London: G. Allen & Unwin.

—— (1980). *A short history of Buddhism.* London and Boston: Allen & Unwin.

Corless, R. (1990). *The vision of Buddhism: The space under the tree.* St. Paul, MN: Paragon House Publishers.

Crossan, J. D. (2009). *Jesus: A revolutionary biography.* New York: HarperCollins Publishers Inc.

Damasio, A. R. (1995). *Descartes' error: Emotion, reason, and the human brain.* New York: Avon Books.

Damasio, A. R., Tranel, D., & Damasio, H. (1990). Individuals with sociopathic behavior caused by frontal damage fail to respond autonomically to social stimuli. *Behavioral and Brain Sciences, 41,* 81-94.

Darwin, C. (1859). *On the origin of species by means of natural selection.* London: J. Murray.

—— (1998). *The expression of the emotions in man and animals.* London: Oxford.

Dawkins, R. (1996). *The blind watchmaker: Why the evidence of evolution reveals a universe without design.* New York: Norton.

—— (2006). *The god delusion*. Boston: Houghton Mifflin Co.

de Ville de Goyet, C. (2004). Epidemics caused by dead bodies: A disaster myth does not want to die. *Rev Panam Salud Publica/Pan Am J Public Health, 15*(5), 297–99

Decaroli, R. (2004). *Haunting the Buddha: Indian popular religions and the formation of Buddhism.* New York: Oxford University Press, Inc.

Diamond, J. M. (1995). *Guns, germs, and steel: The fates of human societies.* New York: W.W. Norton.

Donald, M. (1991). *Origins of the modern mind: Three stages in the evolution of culture and cognition.* Cambridge: Harvard University Press.

Douglas, M. (2003). *Natural symbols: Explorations in cosmology.* London; New York: Routledge.

—— (2005). *Purity and danger: An analysis of concept of pollution and taboo.* London; New York: Routledge.

Dulaney, S., & Fiske, A. P. (1994). Cultural rituals and obsessive-compulsive disorder: Is there a common psychological mechanism? *Ethos, 22*(3), 243–83.

Dunbar, R. (1996). *Grooming, gossip, and the evolution of language.* Cambridge, MA: Harvard University Press.

Durkheim, E. (1951). *Suicide: A study in sociology.* Glencoe, IL.: Free Press.

—— (1976). *The elementary forms of the religious life* (2nd ed.). London: Allen and Unwin.

Durkheim, E., & Lukes, S. (1982). *The rules of sociological method* (1st American ed.). New York: Free Press.

Dutt, S. (2000). *Buddhist monks and the monasteries of India: Their history and their contribution to Indian culture.* Delhi: Motilal Banarsidass.

Earhart, H. B. (1992). *Japanese religion: Unity and diversity.* Wadsworth Publishing.

Eliade, M. (1965). *The myth of the eternal return.* Princeton, NJ: Princeton University Press.

Eliade, M., & Sheed, R. (1996). *Patterns in comparative religion.* Lincoln: The University of Nebraska Press.

Evans-Pritchard, E.E. (1937). *Witchcraft, oracles, and magic among the Azande.* Oxford: Claredon Press.

—— (1956). *Nuer religion.* Oxford: Clarendon Press.

Eysenck, H. J. (1992). The definition and measurement of Psychoticism. *Personality and Individual Difference, 13,* 757–85.

Eysenck, H. J., Eysenck, Sybil B. G. (1994). *Manual of the Eysenck personality questionnaire.* EdITS/Educational and Industrial Testing Service.

Falk, H. (1990). Goodies from India: Literacy, orality, and Vedic culture. In W. Raible (Ed.), *Erscheinungsformen kultureller Prozesse.* (pp. 103–20). Tubingen: Gunter Narr Verlag.

Falk, N. A. (1989). The case of the vanishing nuns: The fruits of ambivalence in ancient Indian Buddhism. In N. A. Falk & R. M. Gross (Eds.), *Unspoken worlds: Women's religious lives.* (pp. 196–206). Belmont, CA: Wadsworth.

Fingarette, H. (1998). *Confucius: The secular as sacred.* Prospect Heights, IL: Waveland Press, Inc.

Fisher, J. (2005). Disposal of dead bodies in emergency conditions. *World Health Organization Technical Notes for Emergencies.* (No. 8), 1–4.

Fiske, A. P., & Haslam, N. (1997). Is Obsessive-Compulsive disorder a pathology of the human disposition to perform socially meaningful rituals? Evidence of similar content. *Journal of Nervous and Mental Disease, 185,* 211–22.

Fogelin, L. (2006). *Archaeology of early Buddhism.* Lanham, MD: AltaMira Press.

Frauwallner, E. (1956). *The earliest Vinaya and the beginnings of Buddhist literature.* Serie Orientale Roma, no. 8. Rome: Instituto Italiano per Il Medio Ed Estremo Oriente.

Frazier, J. G. (1911). *The golden bough: A study in magic and religion.* London: Macmillan.

Geertz, C. (1973). *The interpretation of cultures.* New York: Basic Books.

Germano, D., & Trainer, K. (Eds.). (2004). *Embodying the dharma: Buddhist relic veneration in Asia.* Albany: State University of New York Press.

Gladwell, M. (2005). *Blink: The power of thinking without thinking* (1st ed.). New York: Little, Brown & Co.

Gombrich, R. (1971). *Precept and practice: Traditional Buddhism in the rural highlands of Ceylon.* London: Oxford University Press.

—— (1988). *Theravada Buddhism: A social history from ancient Benares to modern Colombo.* New York: Routledge.

Gomez, L. O. (1987). Buddhism in India. In M. Eliade (Ed.), *Encyclopedia of religion* (Vol. 2, pp. 351–85). London and New York: Macmillan.

Goody, J. (1962). *Death, property and the ancestors: A study of the mortuary customs of the Lodagaa of West Africa.* Stanford, CA.: Stanford University Press.

—— (1987). *The interface between the written and the oral.* Cambridge [Cambridgeshire]; New York: Cambridge University Press.

Gross, R. M. (1993). *Buddhism after patriarchy: A feminist history, analysis, and reconstruction of Buddhism.* Albany: State University of New York Press.

Guthrie, S. E. (1995). *Faces in the clouds: A new theory of religion.* New York: Oxford University Press.

Haidt, J., McCauley, C., & Rozin, P. (1993). Individual difference in sensitivity to disgust. *Personality and Individual Difference,* 701–713.

Hare, R. (1999). *Without conscience: The disturbing world of psychopaths among us.* New York: The Guilford Press.

Harle, J. C. (1994). *The art and architecture of the Indian subcontinent.* New Haven, CT and London: Yale University Press.

Harrison, P. (1987). Who gets to ride in the great vehicle? Self-image and identity among the early Mahayana. *Journal of the International Association of Buddhist Studies, 10* (1), 67–89.

—— (1995). Searching for the origins of the Mahayana: What are we looking for? *Eastern Buddhist, 28*(1), 48–69.

Harvey, P., Baghri, S., & Reed, R.A. (2002). Emergency sanitation, assessment and program design. *WEDC,* Loughborough, UK.

Hertz, R. (1960). A contribution to the study of the collective representation of death (R. Needham & C. Needham, Trans.). In *Death and the right hand*. (pp. 27–86). London: Cohen and West.

Hoffman, J. J., Hall, R. W., & Bartsch, T. W. (1987). On the relative importance of "psychopathic" personality and alcoholism on neuropsychological measures of frontal lobe dysfunction. *Journal of Abnormal Psychology, 96*, 158–60.

Howard, P. (2000). *The owner's manual for personality at work*. Austin, TX: Bard Press.

Howard, P., & Howard, J. M. (2006). *The school place "Big Five" 2.0 professional manual*. Charlotte, NC: Center for Applied Cognitive Studies.

Humphrey, C., & Laidlaw, J. (1994). *The archetypal actions of ritual: A theory of ritual illustration by the Jain rite of worship*. Oxford: Oxford University Press.

Jablonka, E., & Lamb, M. J. (2005). *Evolution in four dimensions: Genetic, epigenetic, behavioral, and symbolic variation in the history of life*. Cambridge: MIT Press.

Jaspers, K. (1953). *The origin and goal of history* (M. Bullock, Trans.). New Haven, CT: Yale University Press.

Johnson, K. (2004). Primary emergence of the doctrinal mode of religiosity in prehistoric southwestern Iran. In H. Whitehouse & L. Martin (Eds.), *Theorizing religions past: Archaeology, history, and cognition*. (pp. 45–68). Walnut Creek, CA: AltaMira Press.

Kegan, R. (1986). The child behind the mask: Sociopathy as developmental delay. In W. H. Reid, D. Dorr, J. I. Walker & J.W. Bonner III. (Eds.), *Unmasking the psychopath*. (pp. 45–77). New York: W. W. Norton.

Kiehl, K. A., Smith, A. M., Hare, R. D., Mendrek, A., Forster, B. B., & Brink, J. (2001). Limbic abnormalities in affective processing by criminal psychopaths as revealed by functional magnetic resonance imaging. *Biological Psychiatry, 50*, 677–84.

Kinney, E., & Gilday, E. T. (2000). Mortuary rites in Japan: Editor's introduction. *Japanese Journal of Religious Studies, 27*(3–4), 163–78.

Klima, A. (2002). *The funeral casino: Meditation, massacre, and exchange with the dead in Thailand*. Princeton, NJ: Princeton University Press.

Koniaris, L. G., McKillop, I. H., Schwartz, S. I., & Zimmers, T. A. (2003). Liver regeneration. *Journal of American College of Surgeons, 197*(4), 634–59.

Kuhn, T. S. (1996). *The structure of scientific revolutions* (3rd ed.). Chicago: The University of Chicago Press.

Kuper, A. (1996). *Anthropology and anthropologists: The modern British school*. New York: Routledge.

Laidlaw, J. (2004). Embedded modes of religiosity in Indic renouncer religions. In H. Whitehouse & J. Laidlaw (Eds.), *Ritual and memory: Toward a comparative anthropology of religion* (pp. 89–109). Walnut Creek, CA: AltaMira Press.

—— (2007). A well-disposed social anthropologist's problems with the "cognitive science of religion." In H. Whitehouse & J. Laidlaw (Eds.), *Religion, anthropology, and cognitive science* (pp. 211–246). Durham, NC: Carolina Academic Press.

Lamotte, E. (1983-84). The assessment of textual authenticity in Buddhism. *The Buddhist Studies Review, 1*(1), 4–15.

—— (1988). *History of Indian Buddhism: From the origins to the Saka era*. Louvain-la-Neuve: Université catholique de Louvain, Institut orientaliste.

Lawson, E. T., & McCauley, R. N. (1990). *Rethinking religion: Connecting cognition and culture*. Cambridge [England]; New York: Cambridge University Press.

Ledoux, J. (1998). *The emotional brain: The mysterious underpinnings of emotional life*. New York: Simon and Schuster.

Leslie, A. M. (1994). Tomm, toby, and agency: Core architecture and domain specificity. In L. A. Hirschfeld & S. A. Gelman (Eds.), *Mapping the mind: Domain specificity in cognition and culture* (pp. 119–48). Cambridge: Cambridge University Press.

Levi-Strauss, C. (1983). *The raw and the cooked: Mythologiques* (Vol. 1). Chicago: The University of Chicago Press.

Lewis, T. T. (2000). *Popular Buddhist texts from Nepal: Narratives and rituals of Newar Buddhism*. Albany: State University of New York Press.

Likert, R. (1932). A technique for the measurement of attitudes. *Archives of Psychology, 22*(140), 1-55.

Ling, T. (Ed.). (1981). *The Buddha's philosophy of man*. London and Rutland: Everyman.

Lopez Jr., D. S. (1995). *Curators of the Buddha: The study of Buddhism under colonialism*. Chicago, IL.: University of Chicago Press.

—— (2001). *The story of Buddhism: A concise guide to its history and teachings* (1st ed.). San Francisco: HarperSanFrancisco.

—— (1995). Authority and orality in the Mahayana. *Numen, 42*(1), 21–47.

Malinowski, B. (1948). *Magic, science, and religion and other essays*. Garden City: The Free Press/Doubleday Anchor Books.

—— (2008/1922). *Argonauts of the western Pacific*. London: Routledge.

McCauley, R. N., & Lawson, E. T. (2002). *Bringing ritual to mind: Psychological foundations of cultural forms*. Cambridge, UK; New York: Cambridge University Press.

McCorkle Jr., W. W. (2008a). Memes, genes, and dead machines: Evolutionary anthropology of death and burial. In J. Bulbulia, R. Sosis, E. Harris, R. Genet, C. Genet & K. Wyman (Eds.), *The evolution of religion: Studies, theories, and critiques* (pp. 287–92). Santa Margarita, CA: Collins Foundation Press.

—— (2008b). The fate of religious studies: The future of an illusion? *Axis Mundi: Slovak Journal for the Study of Religions, 3*(2), 12–18.

—— (forthcoming -a). From corpse to concept: A cognitive theory on the ritualized treatment of dead bodies. In A. W. Geertz (Ed.), *Origins of religion, cognition and culture*. London: Equinox Press LTD.

—— (forthcoming -b) From compulsion to script: The vertical and horizontal transmisson of ritual behavior. In A.W. Geertz (Ed.), *Ritual behavior, cognition and culture*. London: Equinox Press LTD.

—— (forthcoming -c) The measurement of meaning: Emotional contagion, socialization, and the generation of cultural representations. In J.S. Jensen (Ed.), *Meaning in religion, cognition, and culture*. London: Equinox Press LTD.

Meloy, J. R. (1988). *The psychopathic mind: Origins, dynamics, and treatment.* Northvale, NJ: Jason Aronson Inc.

Merrill, M. (2003, 02/12/2007). Monk set himself on fire in protest. [on-line] Retrieved 12/26, 2003, from http://www.le.org/pipermail/vacets-local-dc/2003-December/000130.html.

Metcalf, P., & Huntington, R. (1991). *Celebrations of death: The anthropology of mortuary ritual* (2nd ed.). Cambridge [England]; New York: Cambridge University Press.

Miller, W. I. (1997). *The anatomy of disgust.* Cambridge and London: Harvard University Press.

Mithen, S. J. (1996). *The prehistory of the mind: A search for the origins of art, religion, and science.* London: Thames and Hudson.

—— (2004). From Ohalo to Çatalhöyök: The development of religiosity during the early prehistory of western Asia, 20,000-7,000 BCE. In H. Whitehouse & L. Martin (Eds.), *Theorizing religions past: Archaeology, history, and cognition.* (pp. 17-44). Walnut Creek, CA: AltaMira Press.

Moore, R. (2003). Buddhist monk burns himself in protest. *The Charlotte Observer.* [On-line] Retrieved 10, 2009, from http://www.freerepublic.com/focus/f-religion/1077328/posts

Morgan, O., and Fisher, J. (2004). Infectious disease risk from dead bodies following natural disasters. *Rev Panam Salud Publica/Pan Am J Public Health, 15*(5), 307-12.

Morris, B. (1987). *Anthropological studies of religion: An introductory text.* Cambridge: Cambridge University Press.

Mort, J., & Slone, D. J. (2006). Considering the rationality of ritual behavior. *Method and Theory in the Study of Religion, 18,* 424-39.

MSNBC (2005 (replay)). Inside evil: Jeffrey Dahmer [Television broadcast], Dateline NBC: Crime and Punishment. USA: NBC.

Nattier, J. (1992). The Heart Sutra: A Chinese apocryphal text? *Journal of the International Association of Buddhist Studies,* Vol. *15*(2), 153-223.

Nikam, N. A., & McKeon, R. (1959). *The edicts of Asoka* (N. A. Nikam & R. McKeon, Trans.). Chicago and London: The University of Chicago Press.

Ogawa, S., Lee, T. M., Kay, A. R., & Tank., D. W. (1990a). Brain magnetic resonance imaging with contrast dependent on blood oxygenation. *Proc. Intl. Acad. Sci. USA, 87,* 9868-9872.

—— (1990b). Oxygenation-sensitive contrasts in magnetic resonance image of rodent brain at high magnetic fields. *Magn Reson Med, 14,* 68-78.

Ogawa, S., Tank, D.W., Menon, R., Ellermann, J.M. Kim, S.-G., Merkle, H., & Ugurbil., K. (1992). Intrinsic signal changes accompanying sensory stimulation: Functional brain mapping with magnetic resonance imaging. *Proc. Intl. Acad. Sci. USA, 89,* 5951-55.

Ogawa, S. M., R.S., Tank, D.W., Kim, S.-G., Merkle, H., Ellermann, J.M., & Ugurbil., K. (1993). Functional brain mapping by blood oxygenation level-dependent contrast magnetic resonance imaging. *Biophys J., 64*(3), 803-12.

Ooms, H. (1975). [Review of the book by Robert J. Smith (1974). Ancestor worship in Japan. Stanford, CA: Stanford University Press]. *Japanese Journal of Religious Studies, 2*(4), 317-21.

P.A.H.O. (2003). Unseating the myths surrounding the management of cadavers, *Disaster Newsletter, 93.* Washington, DC: Pan American Health Organization.

—— (2004). Management of dead bodies in disaster situations. *Disaster Manuals and Guideline Series*. Washington, DC: Pan American Health Organization, No. 5, 1-194.

Pals, D. (2006). *Eight theories of religion*. Oxford and New York: Oxford University Press.

Parker Pearson, M. (1999). *The archaeology of death and burial*. College Station: Texas A&M University Press.

Parry, J. (1994). *Death in Banaras*. Cambridge: Cambridge University Press.

Parsons, T. (1993/1922). Introduction. In M. Weber, *The sociology of religion* (pp. xxix-lxxvii). Boston: Beacon Press.

Pennington, M. (2006, Friday, May 5). Quran laid to rest in Pakistani tunnels. *The Charlotte Observer* (AP), p. 20A.

Plath, D. W. (1964). Where the family of god is the family: The role of the dead in Japanese households. *American Anthropologist, 66*(2), 300-317.

Popper, K. (1972). *Objective knowledge: An evolutionary approach*. Oxford: Oxford University Press.

Pyysiäinen, I. (2003). *How religion works: Towards a new cognitive science of religion*. Leiden/Boston: Brill.

Rahula, W. (1974). *What the Buddha taught*. New York: Grove Press.

Rawski, E. S. (1988). A historian's approach to Chinese death ritual. In J. L. Watson & E. S. Rawski (Eds.), *Death ritual in late imperial and modern China* (pp. 20-34). Berkeley and Los Angeles: University of California Press.

Reader, I. (1991). *Religion in contemporary Japan*. Honolulu: University of Hawaii Press.

Reid, W. H. (1986). *Unmasking the psychopath: Antisocial personality and related behaviors*. New York: W.W. Norton and Company.

Rhys-Davids, T. W., & Oldenberg, H. (1996). *Vinaya texts* (Vol. 13). Delhi: Motilal Banarsidass.

—— (1998a). *Vinaya texts* (Vol. 17). Delhi: Motilal Banarsidass.

—— (1998b). *Vinaya texts* (Vol. 20). Delhi: Motilal Banarsidass.

Rhys-Davids, T. W. (1900). *Buddhist Suttas* (Vol. 11). Oxford: Oxford University Press.

Richert, R.R., & Harris, P. L. (2006). The ghost in my body: Children's developing concept of the soul. *Journal of Cognition and Culture, 6* (3-4), 409-27.

Robinson, R. H., & Johnson, W. L. (1982). *The Buddhist religion: A historical introduction* (3rd ed.). Belmont, CA: Wadsworth.

Rozin, P. (1976). The evolution of intelligence and access to the cognitive unconscious. In J.M. Sprague and A. N. Epstein (eds.), *Progress in psychobiology and physiological psychology* (pp. 123-34). Bingley, UK: Emerald Group Publishing Limited.

—— (1997). Disgust faces, basal ganglia and Obsessive-Compulsive disorder: Some strange brainfellows. *Trends in Cognitive Sciences, 1*(9), 321.

Rozin, P., & Fallon, A. (1987). A perspective on disgust. *Psychological Review, 94*, 23-41.

Rozin, P., Haidt, J., & McCauley., C. R. (1993). Disgust. In M. Lewis and J. M. Haviland (Ed.), *Handbook of emotions* (pp. 69-73). New York: Guilford.

Salomon, R., Allchin, F. R., Barnard, M., & British Library. (1999). *Ancient Buddhist scrolls from Gandhara: The British Library Kharosthi fragments.* London: British Library.

Sanford, J. H., Lafleur, W. R., & Nagatomi, M. (Eds.). (1992). *Flowing traces: Buddhism in the literary and visual arts of Japan.* Princeton, NJ: Princeton University Press.

Schaller, M., Duncan, L. A. (In press). *The behavioral immune system: Its evolution and social psychological implications.* New York: Psychology Press.

Schopen, G. (1995). Death, funerals, and the division of property in a monastic code. In D. S. Lopez Jr. (Ed.), *Buddhism in practice* (pp. 473-502). Princeton, NJ: Princeton University Press.

—— (1997). *Bones, stones, and Buddhist monks: Collected papers on the archaeology, epigraphy, and texts of monastic Buddhism in India.* Honolulu: University of Hawai'i Press.

—— (2000). The Mahayana and the middle period of Indian Buddhism: Through the Chinese looking glass. *The Eastern Buddhist, 32*(2), 1-25.

—— (2004). *Buddhist monks and business matters: Still more papers on monastic Buddhism in India.* Honolulu: University of Hawai'i Press.

—— (2005). *Figments and fragments of Mahayana Buddhism in India: More collected papers.* Honolulu: University of Hawai'i Press.

Silk, J. A. (1994). The Victorian creation of Buddhism. *Journal of Indian Philosophy, 22,* 171-96.

Slone, D. J. (2004). *Theological incorrectness: Why religious people believe what they shouldn't.* Oxford; New York: Oxford University Press.

Slone, D. J., & Mort, J. (2005). Sexism vs. superhuman agency in the Theravada Buddhist ritual system. *Method and Theory in the Study of Religion, 17*(2), 134-48.

Smith, J.Z. (2004). *Relating religion: Essays in the study of religion.* Chicago: The University of Chicago Press.

Smith, R. J. (1974). *Ancestor worship in contemporary Japan.* Stanford, CA: Stanford University Press.

Sperber, D. (1975). *Rethinking symbolism.* Cambridge; New York: Cambridge University Press.

—— (1985). *On anthropological knowledge.* Cambridge; Cambridge University Press.

—— (1996). *Explaining culture: A naturalistic approach.* Oxford, UK; Cambridge, Mass.: Blackwell.

—— (2000). *Metarepresentations: A multidisciplinary perspective.* Oxford; New York: Oxford University Press.

Spiro, M. E. (1966). Religion: Problems of definition and explanation. In M. Banton (Ed.), *Anthropological Approaches to the Study of Religion. 3,* 85-126.

—— (1982). *Buddhism and society: A great tradition and its Burmese vicissitudes* (second ed.). Los Angeles and Berkeley: University of California Press.

Staal, F. (1979). The meaninglessness of ritual. *Numen, 26*(1), 2-22.

—— (1989). *Rules without meaning: Ritual, mantras, and the human sciences* (Vol. 4). New York: Peter Lang Publishing, Inc.

Stephen, M. (1988). Devouring the mother: A Kleinian perspective on necrophagia and corpse abuse in mortuary ritual. *Ethos, 26*(4), 387-409.

Strong, J. (2004). *Relics of the Buddha.* Princeton: Princeton University Press.

Swearer, D. K. (1987). Folk Buddhism. In M. Eliade (Ed.), *Encyclopedia of religion* (Vol. 5, pp. 374-8). London and New York: Macmillan.

Swearer, D. K. (2004). *Becoming the Buddha: The ritual of image consecration in Thailand.* Princeton: Princeton University Press.

Tambiah, S. J. (1970). *Buddhism and the spirit cults in north-east Thailand.* Cambridge: Cambridge University Press.

—— (1976). *World conqueror and world renouncer: A study of Buddhism and polity in Thailand against a historical background.* Cambridge: Cambridge University Press.

—— (1984). *The Buddhist saints of the forest and the cult of amulets: A study in charisma, hagiography, sectarianism, and millennial Buddhism.* Cambridge: Cambridge University Press.

Tanabe Jr., G. J. (Ed.). (1999). *Religions of Japan in practice.* Princeton, NJ: Princeton University Press.

Teiser, S. F. (1988). *The ghost festival in medieval China.* Princeton: Princeton University Press.

Trainer, K. (2006). *Relic, ritual, and representation in Buddhism.* Cambridge: Cambridge University Press.

Turner, V. (1995). *The ritual process: Structure and anti-structure.* Hawthorne, NY: Aldine De Gruyter.

Tylor, E. B. (1871). *Primitive culture.* London: Murray.

Van Gennep, A. (1960). *The rites of passage.* Chicago: University of Chicago Press.

Vass, A. A., Smith, R. R., Thompson, C. V., Burnett, M. N., Wolf, D.A., Synstelien, J. A., Dulgerian, N., Eckenrode, B. A. (2004). Decompositional odor analysis database. *Journal of Forensic Science, 49*(4), 760–69.

Watson, J. L. (1982). Of flesh and bones: The management of death pollution in Cantonese society. In M. Bloch & J. Parry (Eds.), *Death and the regeneration of life* (pp. 155–86). Cambridge: Cambridge University Press.

—— (1988a). The structure of funeral rites. In J. L. Watson & E. S. Rawski (Eds.), *Death ritual in late imperial and modern China* (pp. 3–19). Oxford: University of California Press, Ltd.

Watson, J. L., & Rawski, E. S. (Eds.). (1988b). *Death ritual in late imperial and modern China.* Berkeley and Los Angeles: University of California Press.

Watson, R. S. (1988c). Remembering the dead: Graves and politics in southeastern China. In J. L. Watson & E. S. Rawski (Eds.), *Death ritual in late imperial and modern China* (pp. 203–27). Oxford: University of California Press, Ltd.

Weber, M. (1993/1922). *The sociology of religion.* Boston: Beacon Press.

Whitehouse, H. (2004). *Modes of religiosity: A cognitive theory of religious transmission.* Walnut Creek, CA: AltaMira Press.

Whitehouse, H., & Laidlaw, J. (2004). *Ritual and memory: Toward a comparative anthropology of religion.* Walnut Creek, CA: AltaMira Press.

—— (2007). *Religion, anthropology, and cognitive science.* Durham, NC: Carolina Academic Press.

Whitehouse, H., & Martin, L. H. (2004). *Theorizing religions past: Archaeology, history, and cognition.* Walnut Creek, CA: AltaMira Press.

Whitehouse, H., & McCauley, R. N. (2005). *Mind and religion: Psychological and cognitive foundations of religiosity*. Lanham, MD: AltaMira Press.

Williams, P. (1989). *Mahayana Buddhism: The doctrinal foundations*. London & New York: Routledge.

Williams, P., & Tribe, A. (2002). *Buddhist thought: A complete introduction to the Indian tradition*. London and New York: Routledge.

Willis, J. (1985). Nuns and benefactresses: The role of women in the development of Buddhism. In Y. Haddad & E. Findly (Eds.), *Women, religion, and social change* (pp. 59-85). Albany: State University of New York.

—— (1992). Female patronage in Indian Buddhism. In B. S. Miller (Ed.), *The powers of art, Indian patronage in Indian culture* (pp. 46-53). New Delhi: Oxford University Press.

Wilson, G. (1939). Nyakyusa conventions of burial. *Bantu Studies, 13*, 1-31.

Wilson, L. (1996). *Charming cadavers: Horrific figurations of the feminine in Indian Buddhist hagiographic literature*. Chicago: University of Chicago Press.

Wisner B. & Adams, J. (2002). Environmental health in emergencies and disasters, *World Health Organization Technical Notes for Emergencies*. Geneva: WHO.

Zuckerman, M., Kuhlman, D.M., Joireman, J., Teta, P., & Kraft, M. (1993). A comparison of the three structural models of personality: The big three, the big five, and the alternative five. *Journal of Personality and Social Psychology, 65*, 757-68.

Index

TORONTO STUDIES IN RELIGION

Donald Wiebe, General Editor

This series of monographs is designed as a contribution to the scholarly and academic understanding of religion. Such understanding is taken to involve both a descriptive and an explanatory task. The first task is conceived as one of surface description involving the gathering of information about religions, and depth description that provides, on the basis of the data gathered, a more finely nuanced description of a tradition's self-understanding. The second task concerns the search for explanation and the development of theory to account for religion and for particular historical traditions. The series, furthermore, covers the phenomenon of religion in all its constituent dimensions and geographic diversity. Both established and younger scholars in the field have been and will be included to represent a wide range of viewpoints and positions, producing original work of high order at the monograph and major study level.

Although predominantly empirically oriented, the series encourages theoretical studies and even leaves room for creative and empirically controlled philosophical and speculative approaches in the interpretation of religions and religion. Toronto Studies in Religion is of particular interest to those who study the subject at universities and colleges but is also of value to the general educated reader.

For additional information about this series or for the submission of manuscripts, please contact:

Peter Lang Publishing, Inc.
Acquisitions Department
P.O. Box 1246
Bel Air, Maryland 20104-1246

To order other books in this series, please contact our Customer Service Department:

(800) 770-LANG (within the U.S.)
(212) 647-7706 (outside the U.S.)
(212) 647-7707 FAX

or browse online by series at:
WWW.PETERLANG.COM